I DREAM OF YESTERDAY AND TOMORROW

A Celebration of the James Bay Crees

Michael Gnarowski
General Editor

The publisher thanks Dr. Richard Preston for permission to print the story of "Big Skunk and How Wolverine Lost His Mistabeo" and *The Nation* magazine for permission to print "A Blast From the Past, James Bay Style."

National Library of Canada Cataloguing in Publication Data
Main entry under title:
I Dream of Yesterday and Tomorrow: A Celebration of the James Bay Cree
ISBN 0-919614-90-6 (bound) ISBN 1-894908-00-7 (pbk.)
1. Cree Indians—James Bay Region (Ont. and Quebec)
I. Gnarowski, Michael, 1934-

E99.C88123 2001 971.4'115 C2001-901798-7

2000
Canadä

PUBLISHED BY:

THE CREE PROJECT EDITORIAL COMMITTEE
Robert Chitty, President, gordongroup. Project Manager.

Brian Craik, Director of Federal Relations, Embassy of the Cree Nation. Principal liaison for the project with the Grand Council of the Crees.

Michael Gnarowski, Ph.D., General Editor.

Karen Patel, M.A., Early Project and Research Coordinator.

CONTRIBUTORS
David Boult, Brian Craik, Jennifer Latham, Andrew Orkin, Boyce Richardson, Geoff Quaile, Andrew Webster.

RESEARCH
Karen Patel, Heritage Research Associates

EDITING
Jennifer Latham, M.A., Managing Editor
Shelley Henderson
Elizabeth Macfie

PHOTOGRAPHY
Fred Cattroll
Robert Chitty

DESIGN
Royston Neale, Margit Hideg, Nancie Maruscak

ACKNOWLEDGEMENTS
Douglas Cardinal, William Nicholls and *The Nation* magazine, Thom Richardson.

The Grand Council
of the Crees

CREE SCHOOL BOARD

gordonGROUP

Contents

FOREWORD

When this project was conceived, and from the moment of the first planning sessions, it was abundantly clear to all that every care would have to be taken to make this book as authentic as possible in its portrayal of the Crees. The intention, then, was to make the James Bay Crees and their story as accessible as possible to the reader. It was obvious from the outset, in preliminary meetings with interested and knowledgeable individuals, both Cree and others, that great care would have to be exercised not to force the story of the Crees into the tight jacket of earlier notions and beliefs. This became an imperative, and served to define the approach of all those who were called upon to contribute to the project's realization. It helped to guide us in our travels in Cree territories where interviews and much photographic work was undertaken, and the co-operation, way of life, and hospitality of many Cree people were gratefully experienced at first-hand. What fell into place for us was the understanding that the best way to realize a somewhat non-traditional but credible presentation of the James Bay Crees was to make sure that what would be seen and heard in this book would be, as much as possible, in their voice.

Of all the many remarkable and gripping accounts of Canada's Native peoples, there is not one that quite matches the extraordinary historical, social, political, and cultural ups and downs that have marked the epic process of the James Bay Crees—the coastal as well as the inland communities. One must add, at once, that the matter that has gone into the making of this book is taken, in the main, from the Cree people who inhabit the eastern and interior regions of James Bay. It is from these sources that interested readers will learn of a people that has inhabited the James Bay lands some 5,000 years, since the glaciers retreated and the landscape transformed itself into a domain of close to 350,000 square kilometres (135,140 square miles) of subartic forest, rivers, and lakes that has provided sustenance, both physical and spiritual, to a remarkable people.

In a collection of this nature, which has drawn on the experiences and the voices of many individuals and organizations, it is obvious that these opinions and points of view must be seen as belonging to those who have expressed them. A clear note of hardship is sounded, and it is echoed and repeated from the earliest days—and while this serves as a counterpoint to the refrains of a much-loved and respected way of life—it continues to be an everyday experience, generation after generation, in the story of a people adapted to a life determined by nature and its ever-recurring cycles. This is a story of conflict, disappointment, accommodation, and great resilience exemplified, perhaps in an ultra contemporary sense, by the building of a community such as Oujé-Bougoumou. The reader will find the contrasts striking—the image of laundry drying side by side with a newly-stretched pelt outside a regular house, which in turn contrasts with the cone-like structure of poles that appears on the cover and is so typical of traditional Cree habitat. This and many other similar instances exemplify how much has changed and yet how much has remained the same in Cree life.

Finally, and as has been noted earlier, this is a collection intended to give expression to many voices—most of them Cree—most of them engaging those issues, political, social, or environmental that have influenced profoundly many aspects of Cree life. In this sense, this book is a record intended to inform and educate the reader about the concerns, the difficulties that had to be faced, and the adjustments that had to be made by the Cree people, as well as the successes that the James Bay Crees have achieved.

Michael Gnarowski

The Crees of Yesterday and Today

We were a rich people in a rich land, a garden.

Grand Chief Ted Moses
December 2000

The Eeyouch of Eeyou Istchee

The James Bay Crees, or Eeyouch, call their land Eeyou Istchee, which means The People's Land. The Eeyouch of Eeyou Istchee occupy the lands drained by rivers flowing to the east coast of James Bay and southeast coast of Hudson Bay, as well as areas in northern Ontario and in the extreme northern reaches of the St. Lawrence watershed. It is generally believed that the Eeyouch have occupied the boreal forests of northern Quebec for 5,000 years. So far, archeological evidence shows their presence extending back about 3,500 years, but some historians go further and suggest that the Eeyouch were the first people to occupy the northern areas after the last ice sheet retreated, 8,000 or 9,000 years ago.

Living until the mid-20th century as a nomadic hunting and gathering culture, the Crees inhabited a rich and beautiful land. Eeyou Istchee is vast, spread across a land area of 344,854 square kilometres (133,158 square miles). From the time that the Europeans began keeping the first records (in the 17th century) until the 20th century, the Eeyouch probably never numbered more than about 5,000. Today the approximately 12,000 Eeyouch occupy nine communities. On the coast are **Whapmagoostui** (Whale River), on southeast Hudson Bay (known as Great Whale in English and Grande-Baleine in French); **Chisasibi** (Grand River), which was originally situated a few kilometres down river on an island in the mouth of the La Grande River and known then as Fort George; **Wemindji** (Berry Mountain), formerly situated further north and known as Old Factory (in the days of the Hudson's Bay Company, "factory" meant "trading post"); **Eastmain** (the name formerly given to the whole east coast of James Bay); and **Waskaganish** (Little House), formerly called Rupert House. Inland are **Nemaska** (Good Fishing Place), **Waswanipi** (Shimmering Water), **Oujé-Bougoumou** (The Water's Source Lake), and **Mistissini** (Big Rock).

80°
66°
57°
49°
HUDSON BAY
WHAPMAGOOSTUI
CHISASIBI
Labrador
WEMINDJI
EASTMAIN
JAMES BAY
MISTISSINI
NEMASKA
WASKAGANISH
Ontario
OUJÉ-BOUGOUMOU
WASWANIPI
St. Lawrence River
Val d'Or

The Path of the Giant Beaver

One Eeyou sacred story tells of a child who was born in an unnatural way and who eventually married a beaver and lived with the beavers, teaching them how to hide from humans.

Later, his human brother found him and he was given a chance to live with the people, but to do so he had to observe a food taboo—never to eat the flesh of a female beaver. One day, someone made him eat that food without his knowing it, and so he left the people by jumping into the river, where he instantly became a giant beaver.

All of the river ice broke as he swam downstream to escape, pursued by his brother. The trail of the chase led from Mistissini toward Oujé-Bougoumou and Waswanipi, down the Rupert River, out into James Bay and then up the coast to Hudson Bay, to the lands of the people of Whapmagoostui.

In a metaphorical way, this story serves to define Eeyou Istchee. All along the route of the chase are well-known landmarks that refer back to this magical moment in Cree prehistory.

Some speakers say Eeyou Istchee while others say Eeyou Astchee. Inland Crees tend to say Eenou, while those on the coast say Eeyou. To avoid confusing readers, Eeyou Istchee is used throughout this book.

In days gone by Mistissini was sometimes known as Mistassini, but the spelling was changed by the Crees to its current form.

Linguistically the Eeyouch are referred to as belonging to the Cree language grouping of the Algonquian family of languages. Algonquian languages are spoken as far south as North Carolina around the Great Lakes and as far west as the Rocky Mountains. The Eeyouch are somewhat linguistically diversified according to a north-south distinction that starts around the present community of Eastmain. People from there northwards tend to use an "a" sound (as in sat) where those south of them would use an "e" sound (as in sell). Similarly people from the north have differences in certain verb endings. These dialectical differences distinguish the communities from one another and are not just reflective of word choice, such as "ostitaskw" for axe in Waswanipi/Oujé-Bougoumou/Mistissini versus "chikhigan" on the coast, but also consist of grammatical differences. There is no simple way of linguistically dividing the Eeyouch; one might say that they are united in their penchant to play with their language.

In the not-too-distant past, an Eeyou, when asked where he or she was from, would often refer to a lake or a river a hundred kilometres or more from any modern-day town or village. The place where a person was born is referred to as that person's eetawin, the "place where they came into being." This term also now refers to a modern-day community—an eetawin is "a place for being." Today, most Crees are born in one of the nine communities, but those who choose to live in the traditional manner spend a large part of their time on their extended family hunting grounds, as their ancestors did.

The southern part of Eeyou Istchee was until recently covered by a mixed pine and spruce forest interspersed with stands of birch, tamarack, poplar, willow, and cedar, depending on the terrain and the number of years since it was last burned over. Logging operations are now reducing this forest at the rate of about 800 square kilometres per year. Farther north, the trees are smaller and more widely spaced, underlain by deep layers of moss. Toward the James Bay coast the land tends to be flat and covered with muskeg, a word of Cree origin that refers to a chain of small bogs. Inland the land rises, so the rivers tend to run east to west. As one progresses north along the coast, the land rises and becomes rockier. The landscape around Whapmagoostui was scoured by a glacier relatively recently. Deposits of gravel and sand, interspersed among rock outcrops, are cut by fast-flowing rivers. Landscapes in the Great Whale and Little Whale River valleys are among the most spectacular in North America.

These northern lands are home to the largest herd of barren ground caribou in the world—comprising about 700,000 animals. The northern rivers are full of trout and sometimes char. Moose seem to be moving northwards (it was only about 20 years ago that a hunter from Whapmagoostui killed the first moose in that area). This migration is likely due to climate change and loss of habitat due to logging and the creation of hydro-electric reservoirs. South of the La Grande River, the land is forested and thus home to beaver, muskrat, mink, marten, lynx, fox, moose, woodland caribou, and bear. The Eastmain River is the northerly limit of sturgeon, walleye and pike are common in the rivers towards the southern James Bay coast, while inland one finds speckled and lake trout in the Mistissini area.

All along the James Bay coast are islands, most of which are rocky, bearing only stunted trees. Some of the larger islands, such as Charlton Island, have inland lakes and streams and diverse habitats where the Eeyouch pick berries and trap beaver, muskrat, fox, and lynx. They also fish and hunt waterfowl and seal on and around these islands.

All of this land and its wildlife have sustained the Eeyouch, who in return recognize that they have a responsibility to protect the land that is both their store and their garden.

As children, we mimicked the activities of our parents. I remember hunting little birds with a slingshot or bow and arrow, as our children do now.

During the summer, we would rise in the morning and return in the evening, completely exhausted after a day of hunting. We would give our quarry to the elders in the camp, pretending the small oschipsheeshich (horned larks) and the wapeeye-cosheeshich (snow buntings) were Canada geese.

This is what defined us, and it was just a short step into the activities of adulthood.

Grand Chief Ted Moses

Ntoho Eeyouch
A Harvesting People

Over thousands of years of coexisting with nature, the Crees have developed and refined a unique system of land and resource management. Unlike most peoples of the world, for the Eeyouch the age-old problem of making a living did not involve the enforcement of clear land boundaries. Crees traditionally organize their hunting activities on the land along family and kinship lines. Each family or group returns to the same hunting or fishing grounds year after year. This does not exclude other families from using these areas; however, they need to get permission from the ouchimaw (tallyman) for access to the territory. ("Tallyman" is the English term used to describe the ouchimaw, and comes from the acquired role of tallying up the furs to be brought to the fur trader. The English term has a pejorative meaning of subservience, and, for this reason, the Cree term will be used in this book.) It is the ouchimaw's responsibility to ensure that recent hunting has not depleted the fish and game on a family's territory, that there is enough to support the group. In modern terms, the ouchimaw is the equivalent of a resource manager or game warden, determining where and when hunting can occur and who can harvest how much.

The hunting families' traditional round of activities varied depending upon where they hunted and fished. It is likely that in prehistoric times, groups of families involving perhaps two or three hundred people got together during the spring at the best sites for hunting waterfowl or fishing. After the fish had spawned, these people moved elsewhere, in groupings of three or four families (groups were larger in the north), to hunt moose, caribou, beaver, and other animals. In the summer, the people of Whapmagoostui hunted the beluga whale, and used its oil and meat throughout the summer. Establishing their tigwatchtawugamukw (autumn house), the Crees fished, snared hares, or caught other game until the lakes froze. Then, the beaver hunters were free to travel far in search of

Beaver have always been trapped in the winter, when their fur is thick and in good condition. One elder described the winter hunting of beaver as being a family occasion.

Sometimes we would find a lodge where it would be very good for catching the beaver in a net. Eschaniw, we called it. We would all go. First we would stop up all of the beaver dens along the riverbank, then we would block up the doors at the beaver lodge with poles going into the bottom of the river. At the main door we would place a net so that if beavers came out, they would slide right into it. It was not easy; you had to be fast to pull up the net bag just at the right time. Everyone used to help. The children would beat on the beaver lodge to get them to come out! Now we don't do this too often. Perhaps some do it, but today people usually use the steel traps where we used to set the net.

Charlie Blackned
Hunter/Trapper

beaver lodges. The caribou hunters in the north also moved in search of the herds and, when they found them, got together in large groups to hunt and then process the hides and meat.

The problem was knowing where the animals would be plentiful and where to find other people in case of sickness or starvation. The knowledge of the elders was valuable because they knew where animals and resources had been found in the past and they also had a social and historical knowledge that extended beyond the experience of most other people.

With such vast areas in which to seek food, the Eeyouch walked great distances, pulling toboggans loaded with their possessions and provisions. It was not unheard of for people to walk a hundred miles in search of game. One who walked far would sometimes refer to the experience as "playing with one's legs."

Material culture was dispensable. To be an Eeyou meant to be able to create what was needed, when it was needed, and from whatever was at hand. People were constantly searching for raw materials and were always working to dry and store food for times when it would not be available.

There have been many changes in the Crees' way of life over the past century, including the development of permanent communities. However family hunting territories, with their customs of use and the resource-management role of the ouchimaw, remain as a cornerstone of Cree culture. Today, Eeyou Istchee is divided into 320 extended-family hunting territories, which vary in size from 200 to 600 square kilometres (77 to 232 square miles) or more. The average size decreases toward the south. These lands are called "harvesting lands" (ntoho istchee) in the south and "beaver lands" (amisk istchee) in the north. This difference is probably because the people of the Chisasibi and Whapmagoostui areas, in the north, originally spent most of their time hunting caribou and did not divide the territory into beaver lands until after the arrival of the fur trade. Whapmagoostui is the only Cree community with a large hunting commons (a large undivided area where any community member can hunt) in the heart of the caribou pasture around Lake Bienville (Apishigameesh—the "little sea"). In the south, while the boundaries of these hunting lands are not fixed for all time, particular areas are associated with and owned by certain families.

Playing With One's Legs

One man in Chisasibi recounted a story of when he was about 15 years old and his father sent him to get matches at Fort Mackenzie, near Ungava Bay. He walked for three days, through an area he had never seen, following his father's verbal instructions.

Another man described how, in 1972, he and his friend decided one winter to go for a walk. Since he could not speak English, he did not know the name of the place they visited, but after some description of what it looked like, it became evident that it was Goose Bay, Labrador, several hundred miles from their lands.

Only a few years ago, one elderly couple decided to walk in the winter from their lands near Waskaganish to Nemaska. As they pulled their toboggans along the side of the road, a young man passing by in his truck offered them a lift. "No," they said, "we are going to set camp tonight and snare some hares." They arrived a week later in Nemaska. Their life was the walk!

In 1999, a group of young and middle-aged Eeyouch walked in winter from Whapmagoostui down the coast to Waskaganish and then from Waskaganish inland to Mistissini, a distance of several hundred miles. They walked to raise money for a dialysis machine to help those suffering from the diabetes epidemic that is sweeping the communities.

*We called them then,
and we still call them,
Wemistigusheeyouch—the
Shaped-Wood People—after
the curiously made craft that
they arrived in.*

Grand Chief Ted Moses

Wemistigusheeyouch
The Shaped-Wood People

When the English first stumbled into Hudson Bay and James Bay in 1610, it was not furs they were looking for but a gateway to the Pacific Ocean. The Eeyouch probably already knew that the Europeans also wanted furs, since several years earlier the Eeyouch had been to Tadoussac, Quebec, in the summer, along with hundreds of neighbouring Algonquian-speaking Aboriginal people, to trade their beaver pelts to the fur-hungry French fishermen and explorers.

The furs, principally beaver, were luxury items for the English, transformed into felt to make men's top hats. For the Crees, the European goods they received in exchange for this most ordinary of commodities were important labour-saving devices: iron axes, chisels, knives, and cooking pots; twine for netting; and cloth for lighter clothing and blankets.

The Crees tell a story today about how a husband and wife approached a ship, described as a floating island with a tall tree in the middle, and were invited aboard. Once on the ship, they were implored to take off their clothes, which were made of muskrat furs. They were given European clothing to wear home. Another story, recorded by an Englishman on a ship icebound in Rupert Bay in 1611, tells of how Cree hunters came onboard and eagerly traded a few beaver pelts for a knife, a looking glass, and buttons. They returned the next day with more furs to trade for a hatchet. Clearly, the fur trade was of interest to both Crees and Europeans.

When the English returned to James Bay to trade, 60 years later, about 300 Cree people turned out to greet them and trade with them. Thus convinced of the potential of profitable trade, merchants in England founded the Hudson's Bay Company in 1670. Its first post was Rupert House, located at the site of present-day Waskaganish. Over the next 150 years, the Company expanded to almost 400 posts throughout Canada's vast northlands, then called "Rupert's Land" by the British.

From the beginning, the Eeyouch incorporated the newcomers into their society. They recognized the trading post as belonging to the Company and accorded the traders lands on which to cut wood and hunt. The Eeyouch referred to the trading post leader as ouchimaw, the word used for the leader of an Eeyou hunting camp.

As the fur trade developed, the Eeyouch continued their way of life in the bush and maintained a large measure of independence from the laws of European and European-derived Canadian societies. The Eeyouch not only traded furs, they also supplied the food required to operate the posts. Yes, the terms of the trade were lopsided in favour of European society (in that the value of the furs far surpassed the value of the goods received by the Eeyouch), but no, the Eeyouch were never servants of the Company. Outside of the little parcels of land occupied by the posts, the laws of the Eeyouch largely ran affairs. Punishments, marriages, and decisions respecting the well-being of the group—all were decided by the Eeyouch, as they always had been. In the 19th century, the Hudson's Bay Company allowed its employees to marry local people. Of course, such marriages happened before that time, but the Company did not recognize them. Also, some Eeyouch took up employment for a few months or for longer periods at the posts. Gradually, resident populations of carpenters, sawyers, farmers, and labourers grew up around the posts. The Company referred to these communities as the Home Guard.

Traditionally, the families who hunted on the coast were associated with nearby rivers that fed into James Bay. In the fall and winter they would follow the river courses inland in search of caribou and other game. In many cases their hunting territories were immense, stretching from the coast to far inland. Within their communities, the Eeyouch differentiate between the Winnigegoweeyouch, or "coasters," and Notchimeeweeyouch "inlanders." The distinction of coaster versus inlander picked up a pejorative meaning during the time of the fur trade as, after freeze-up, the sick and aged would be left on the coast with a young hunter, who would trap foxes and trade for supplies at the post, while the most able in the community would go inland to seek caribou and other game. In this way the "coaster" term came to be associated with more reliance on the trading post.

When the Europeans first began to come across an ocean to trade with us, we integrated fur trading into our economy and activities.

In socio-economic and human rights terminology, we enjoyed our own means of subsistence and production.

Grand Chief Ted Moses

Ateeyoucan Keeyeh Eeyou Eetowin
Sacred Stories and Beliefs of the Eeyouch

The pre-Christian beliefs of the Eeyouch, which remain part of their culture, recognize the balance of nature and how people fit into this spiritual and physical world. Their traditional laws of nature and spirituality reveal their deep respect for maintaining a harmonious relationship with nature.

- *Mother Earth provides for and nurtures everything. Therefore, Mother Earth must be loved and honoured.*
- *When something is taken from Mother Earth, something must be given back.*
- *It is the responsibility of all peoples to protect and preserve the land.*
- *Water is sacred and is life-giving.*
- *All peoples must live in harmony with the natural order.*
- *There is medicine on the land, where beauty and strength can be found.*
- *Human life is one with Creation.*
- *Sacred and natural laws govern all of Creation.*
- *Knowledge comes from the Creator through the land.*
- *Life is tied to and connected to the land.*
- *Peoples must acknowledge, give thanks for, and honour what is received and taken from the land.*
- *Everything has a spirit.*
- *Eeyouch and all the peoples of the world are connected to the spirit of the land.*

Learning to achieve balance is an essential part of growing up. A person is taught not to attempt to exceed his or her capabilities. However, because life can be demanding and sometimes requires superhuman effort, each person walks a fine line to maintain his or her personal equilibrium.

In Eeyou society, people understood the physical world through traditions, which everyone had access to. Tradition included the mundane, sometimes called the "tough way of doing things," from knowing how to tie a knot to being able to make snowshoes. It was believed that if a camp was run well, the people in that camp would be protected from misfortune. The details of tradition extended into how food was cut up and served, how the bones were disposed of afterwards, and even how one spoke and thought about the animals, other people, and nature.

Even here, balance came in. The importance of practising the traditions with ease and grace was recognized. And it was recognized that certain people had a talent for these things. The problem was that sometimes even the best practitioners of their culture do not succeed. Being able to make a perfect snare was not a guarantee that the hare would be caught. When an Eeyou hunter could not bring home game, people went hungry and sometimes starved. For this reason, the correct attitude for the hunter was one of gratitude and recognition that success was determined by a world of complex factors. Too much success, such as catching two animals in one trap, could be a message that a loved one far away had died or was dying. This was called ehpaweeyeitik—to receive knowledge, in a spiritual way, of another's misfortune. When someone did not have success in hunting, this person was ehpishhot—cut off from his or her relationship with nature. A person in this situation would sometimes look around for the cause. Was it someone in the camp? Was it someone far away? Was it an error in ritual and in the respect shown for the animals?

In the traditional society, the elders were the ones who taught the traditions and insisted on their observance. They held the responsibility of keeping alive the memory, history, and knowledge of the Eeyou ancestors. Their sharing of life experiences and stories helped the people make decisions. The elders were the voices of moderation, experience, and guidance.

The Crees also believed that some people could read the spiritual forces at play in nature. While some people knew little of this, others seemed more perceptive and able to ride on the crest of good fortune through life. This Eeyou ideal, ehmitewatseet, referred to someone who was able to ride the ebb and flow of life without trying to dominate or control events or other people too much. It was also recognized that there were those who seemed to have the spiritual power to control events, manipulating outcomes and people. These people, called the miteoch, were much feared.

All animals and plants, all natural forces are personalized in the Cree mind and spoken of in the Cree language in the personal form. These natural forces make decisions, just as people do; and if their personal qualities are not respected, they can make life impossible for the hunter. For example, chuetenshu, the north wind, gives the animals to the Indians in January by making the snow accumulate to such a depth that the moose's belly drags and the hunters can easily catch him .... But chuetenshu can be capricious, like any person, and when he brings weather that is too cold, the snow hardens and the Indian's snowshoes make such a clatter on the crust that the moose is warned of his coming and is hard to catch .... Everything in nature behaves in this complex way.

Boyce Richardson
From Strangers Devour the Land

The knowledge of the elders was fascinating to us. They told stories from the past and recounted legends. They had knowledge of inland places hundreds of miles away that few in our community had ever seen. Their understanding of the animals and of animal behaviour was valuable to everyone and fascinating to us children.

Our heroes were the figures in the stories told by the elders—stories of the one who could run down caribou on snowshoes, who survived incredible famine, who walked hundreds of miles, and who knew the animals like no other human being.

Grand Chief Ted Moses

Being isolated in the bush for months at a time made people worry about the health of loved ones far away. If someone in the camp knew how to make a shaking tent, this person could be consulted. With a shaking tent, a person could ask the spirits how others were keeping, find out where the animals might be, or ask for help to cure the sick. For the ritual, a tent was made of newly cut poles, put into the ground in a circle, and covered with canvas or hide. The kosapituk—a person who could communicate with the spirits—would enter the tent, and sing and call on his spiritual helper (often a bear) to help him find others. It is said that the spirits who had been called would come in and sit around in the top of the tent. The audience waiting and listening outside the tent would ask questions about the well-being of loved ones or about the whereabouts of game, and tuck a gift of tobacco under the canvas. They could hear the voices of the animals and speakers inside and see the tent shake. This performance might last several hours. The kosapituk was not necessarily seen as someone evil but as someone with a gift that they could not deny. However, others might view these powers with fear and see them as a potential means of doing evil.

Eeyou beliefs can also be understood through the legends and stories by which the people passed on their history and traditional teachings. A set of sacred stories, called atiokan, explained (among other things) the origin of the separation of animals and man and the origin of the seasons. The story of the man who turned into a giant beaver is one such atiokan. Other atiokan tell tales of Wolverine and Big Skunk and of how Wolverine lost his spirit friend, Mistabeo. These transformation legends, like the story of Big Skunk and Wolverine that follows this Introduction, provide symbolic insight into the ability of the Eeyouch to stand against large foes and to transform themselves in order to handle the events that affect them and their land.

Today, almost all Eeyouch have knowledge of these traditional ways and sacred beliefs, and many have experienced these practices first-hand. Many Eeyouch follow these traditions rather than, or in addition to, Christianity.

Ayimhewin
Religion

In the 19th century, the Methodists came to the James Bay area and introduced Christianity to the Crees, but they did not stay. After them came the Anglicans, who established missions. By the late 1800s and early 1900s, life had changed enough for the Crees, due to epidemics of European origin, declining caribou and beaver numbers, and increased wage labour at the posts, that they accepted this new religion alongside their own traditional one. To some extent, it fit into the existing Cree view of the world. The personal nature of Christian salvation, and the concept of Christian faith as a protector against hard times, fit well with the Cree view of the individual's role in making the universe unfold as it should. People tried to blend aspects of the new and the old religions. Some saw the sacrifices in the Old Testament as a vindication of the Eeyou practice of ehmitchtehamanot (burning meat for the spirits). The church did, however, frown on this and on ehmitekitawewin (the controlling of events to dominate or punish others) and other Eeyou beliefs, such as the shaking tent ritual.

Since the early 1970s, some Eeyouch in the southern communities have taken up the Evangelical Baptist and Pentecostal faiths. Many of these people consider the Anglican church, like the old Eeyou beliefs, too focused on empty or mal-intentioned ritual. They seek a faith in which the prayers of the believers can affect present events. They also seek a religion that requires the individual to commit personally and daily to the observance of certain meaningful practices, such as daily prayer, abstention from alcohol, and daily study of the gospel.

Today the communities of Eastmain, Wemindji, Chisasibi, and Whapmagoostui have congregations of the Anglican faith. The other communities still have small congregations of Anglicans, and they also have larger Pentecostal and some Evangelical Baptist congregations. All communities have a number of people who profess the traditional religion. Indeed, most people have come to understand Christianity in terms of their own culture. Also, in most communities, a number of people have introduced philosophical and religious views based on Native American beliefs from the western United States and Canada, attempting to combine traditional Eeyou beliefs with those based on prophesies from other Native American cultures.

Why are the Eeyouch called the Crees?

When Christianity was introduced to the Eeyouch, they found that aspects of it fit in with their own belief system.

Some say that the name "Cree" derives from a shortening of the way the Eeyouch and other Aboriginal peoples referred to them—as the "Chreestianaux" or "Christians."

Ancheesh Eytitaw Eeyouch
The Eeyouch in the 20th Century

With the coming of the White man and the fur trade, the availability of European goods rendered certain traditional skills obsolete. The ability to work stone into points, manufacture wooden traps, and build bark canoes and containers gradually decreased in importance and in practice. Nevertheless, though widespread knowledge of these skills declined through lack of use, well into the 20th century people continued to live in the

bush with few possessions other than what they had made themselves. Up until the late 1950s, people went into the bush for months at a time, carrying only twine for nets, matches, a rifle, ammunition, sewing materials, canvas, a few utensils, knives, some tea, sugar, perhaps some lard, and their clothing. Today, most Eeyou individuals continue to practise some or many traditional skills. About one third of the adults are dependant on the bush as their primary way of making a living and others continue to spend many weeks of the year in the bush. It is often said that some of those who work in jobs today work in order to support their hunting as, most of the time, their thought and money goes toward this activity. The Eeyouch are still very much the Ntoho Eeyouch.

In the early part of the century, when airplanes arrived in the north and schools were built in the communities, the strategy of earning a living in the bush changed for many people. Some members of the family could fly in and out of remote bush locations, while others would stay in town with grandparents or other relatives. Material needs in town had to be met. From the money they earned trading furs, people bought modern conveniences, such as outboard motors, gas stoves, and washing machines. Even so, the staple of life at that time was still the two million pounds of meat that the Eeyouch harvested annually from Eeyou Istchee.

Mistamisk Ehbej-Cheewet-Oskotamchesiw
The Return of the Giant Beaver—Hydro-Québec

In the early 1970s, the Eeyouch received the shocking news that their land—the basis for their way of life—was to become the site of one of the world's largest hydroelectric complexes: the James Bay Project. The project called for the diversion of various rivers, the building of dams, and the flooding of thousands of square kilometres of land. The first phase of the hydroelectric project brought roads that also opened the territory to increased mining and extensive cutting of the forests.

This book tells of the heroic efforts of the Eeyouch to preserve what was theirs and of their endeavours to develop their society in the face of rapid change. The voices of the people bring to life what most Canadians saw only flashes of in the newspapers or on television. This is a story of mythic proportions—a story about political battles to save a homeland, in which the Eeyouch have defined a unique relationship with Canada and Quebec, and about a population swiftly adapting to the modern world while struggling to remain Eeyou.

Photo of John Blackned, circa 1960s.

Mythic Beginnings

For the Crees, storytelling is an oral tradition passed from one generation to another. Stories are memorized and repeated, sometimes changing each time they are told. They incorporate all that life incorporates, accepting good and evil, cruelty and beauty, crudeness and fancy equally, as part of the world.

Storytellers are judged according to their eloquence, and their ability to improvise and improve stories for entertainment. Crees tell long stories about personal hunting adventures, using gestures and motions to illustrate the movements of the animals, the stealthy approach of the hunter, the aim, the shot, the cry of the animal.

Cree sacred stories, atiokan, explain the mythic beginnings and mysterious origins of such things as the seasons and the arrival of humans on the land. Crees often personify animals and nature in their stories, giving human-like qualities, abilities, and personalities to the animal and land characters—animals and trees talk to each other, and animals use spears and bows to fight their enemies. Keenly attuned to the cycle of nature, Crees understand that change and transformation are part of their relationship with the animals and the land on which they depend. It is not therefore surprising that transformation and change are sometimes themes of their atiokan.

The connection to nature, the spirits, and other peoples is part of Cree culture and is reflected in the stories that are told to children from the time they are born. Stories are used to entertain listeners of all ages and to instruct the young. They are also used to preserve history, rituals, and beliefs.

Stories often lose meaning when translated from their original language. Meaning is also often lost when the stories are told to people of other cultures. There are images, suggestions, and associations that mean nothing to the outsider but that are apparent to the Crees. The story of "Big Skunk and How Wolverine Lost his Mistabeo" tells of two important events: a battle with a great foe and how the arrival of human neighbours transforms the lives of the animals. The cunning of the animals leads them to victory over their enemy, but the nature of their existence must change with the coming of humans. These ancient events have great meaning for the Crees, and can even be seen to reflect the modern battles faced by the James Bay Crees as they must transform and adapt to the changes to their lives and lands.

(Adapted from the Web site of the Canadian Museum of Civilization)

The Story of "Big Skunk and How Wolverine Lost His Mistabeo"

Written and recorded by Dr. Richard Preston

Dr. Richard Preston, McMaster University, has sojourned and worked with the people of the James Bay region, learning about their traditional ecological knowledge in order to trace the emergence of the Cree concept of community. In his journeys among the Crees he was able to record the story of "Big Skunk and How Wolverine Lost His Mistabeo."

We will begin our entry into the Cree myth of their original frontier with a story that relates what some animal-persons did, and how they lived and talked together, before there were human beings on the scene. Some of the animals gathered to form a community, with a leader—Wolverine. Part of their reason for living together was for mutual support in protecting themselves against strange, threatening outsiders.

As we will see, the threats are all too real, and this original community struggles for its life. At first, they succeed against a fierce enemy, but their success does not carry them through a less threatening but very strange new kind of creature from beyond the frontier—human beings.

Humans arrive and soon become the custodians of community. The animals lose their ability to live with and talk to each other. As we will see, their community is lost as much through a failure of leadership as through the damaging effects of the human strangers. And, as we will also see, the universal human tendency to appeal to spiritual persons for help is a part of this primal, mythic community.

We will begin, then, at the mythic beginning as it was told by John Blackned of Waskaganish in 1964, 1965, and 1979. In order to get the most out of the story of Giant Skunk, an introduction to some of the persons or personalities of the story is essential.

Mistabeo: a spiritual being, literally meaning "great man" but actually referring to a person who has no visible body but who may choose to ally himself with a man. Mistabeo is able to tell what will happen in the future or what is happening far away. He is also sometimes able to accomplish extraordinary feats of strength in struggling with dangerous beings, sometimes called devils. He is not omniscient or omnipotent; he just has greater-than-human abilities.

Wolverine: a solitary hunting animal, about the size of a medium-sized dog, and built a bit like a bear. He has a reputation for stealing traps and trapping tools, and spoiling a trapper's camp by tearing things apart or stealing them. Tough, mean-minded, and aggressive, he is regarded as antisocial. His fur, however, is the best for trimming a parka hood; very warm and slow to accumulate frost from one's breath. Many animals may rob traps; only this one also likes to steal the trap itself. He can ruin a trapper.

Skunk: a small but voracious hunter whose musk is to be avoided and is very difficult to wash off. He is capable of spraying this musk with fair aim, from an opening adjacent to his anus, at any creature that he dislikes. He has few enemies but also few friends.

Lynx, or Bobcat: a little larger than Wolverine, and more common. He is not aggressive like Wolverine or Skunk. He likes to eat rabbits, who fear his smell so much that the Crees used to smear lynx dung on their leather-thong snares for rabbits because the rabbit, smelling the lynx, will not try to gnaw through the thong and escape from the snare.

Marten: smaller than Skunk, quick, curious, and mischievous. Marten traps are concealed with a jumble of boughs because the unnatural appearance of the jumble will attract his attention and make him curious to find out why this should look so strange. You could say that Marten sometimes traps himself because of his curiosity.

Rabbit: unlike the others described above, he is not a hunter but an eater of plants, whose survival in a world of hunters is in his timidity and ability to run quickly when he suspects a threat. He is not at all clever and, like the caribou, will risk a snare rather than go off his beaten path.

Frog: neither a hunter nor a plant eater, he eats insects. His skin is without fur, and he survives the winter by burying himself in mud. He is shaped unlike anything else, and is regarded as untouchable by the Crees. Having no satisfactory form in the animal world, Frog is said to want to sleep next to humans, to become like them. You might want to check your bed from time to time.

The story as told by John Blackned:

Before the human beings came, all the animals spoke the same language. Mistabeo found the land. He gathered all the animals, including the Wolverine. He could not find humans at that time, so he found Wolverine to conjure with. He told them what was going to happen later on: "When the human beings arrive, they will kill us for their meat," he said. "All of us will be killed and all of us will be their meat. And when humans arrive, Mistabeo will go to them; they will have Mistabeo."

The animals gathered together and they talked about trying to be humans, themselves, so they wouldn't be killed. Wolverine said, "The human will have wives, and we are going to have wives. There is going to be a lot of humans." Wolverine told them that he will ask Mistabeo to have a kwashapshig-an (make a conjuring tent that Wolverine and Mistabeo will go into to find out the news of what is going to happen) and Mistabeo said, "All right. And when the human beings arrive I won't bother you again."

And so they were making plans to be human, and Wolverine said, "I have got a Mistabeo, now." (He doesn't accept what Mistabeo said, that he would leave him.) So Lynx also said that he will try to be a human, and his wife was Marten. He decided to marry Marten because the Marten climbs trees, and he also likes to climb. Rabbit also said that he will be a human, and he was told that he will be the one that will be chased and killed all the time. Because of this, he decided to have a wife that could jump like him, so he found the small, green, fast jumping Frog. (Foolish Rabbit!)

In these far-off times, Skunk was much bigger than he is today. His widui (scent glands) were so powerful they would kill. So at that time, the animals were gathered together to live in one tent because of their fear of the Big Skunk. And they thought of themselves as the humans of that time. These animals were Wolverine, Fisher, Lynx, Weasel, Squirrel, Marten, Rabbit and the others that run

in the forest. Even when Skunk is far off, if an animal crosses its trail, it knows what is happening because its widui quivers inside his body. The widui quivers a little bit differently if the animal is far away than if the animal is close. No matter how far away, if Skunk feels his widui quiver, he gets mad at whoever is crossing his trail and he turns back to kill that person. If the animals know that this is Skunk's trail, they would back away from it.

They gathered under one tent from fear of the Big Skunk, and they tried to think of a way to get rid of this Skunk. Wolverine was the boss of the animals; he has a Mistabeo. He called the others his "little brothers" because he thinks more of himself. He told them not to cross the Skunk's trail. But it was Weasel, because he is especially curious, that crossed the trail. He wondered what Skunk's trail looked like, and he thought that if he burrowed under the snow and just came up beside the trail, maybe that would be safe. So that is what he did. Wolverine had not seen the Skunk's trail when he came back to the tent, and he asked his little brothers. Weasel was expecting trouble for what he did, so he didn't answer right away. But already Skunk had started for them. Finally, Weasel told how he had seen the trail. So the animals knew they had to try to save themselves, and they left the place and travelled all day. They made a camp for the night, and at that time, Skunk reached their old place.

In the morning they started out, but Skunk was still on their trail. Wolverine told his little brothers that Skunk would catch up to them that day. There was a lake near where they stopped and got ready. Wolverine told his little brothers to take their spears and hide themselves on both sides of the trail. Then Wolverine dug himself a hole in the snow at the end of their trail and hid himself. He told them that he was going to try to bite the opening where Skunk's widui shoots out, but the other animals doubted if he could do it. They thought that this would be the end of them. Then Skunk came up, and knew that they were there. "Why are you travelling such great distances?" he asked. And Wolverine answered, "It is because of your widui that everybody has to go as far away as possible." Wolverine was peeking out of his hole, and Skunk told him, "Why don't you look at me, face to face?"

Wolverine stuck his head up, and right away Skunk whirled around backwards to shoot his widui at Wolverine. But Wolverine was very quick and he sprang up and got his teeth into Skunk's behind, clamping down the opening so that the liquid could not come out. This was the signal for the others and Wolverine shouted (but you could hardly hear him), "I've got the opening!" through his teeth. The others said, "Our brother is shouting!" They came running and found that Wolverine was managing to hang on to Skunk's opening.

With their spears they started stabbing the Skunk, and finally he toppled over. And their brother fell with him, but he still hung on. Then Skunk didn't move at all; they knew he was dead then. And Wolverine was still hanging on when he said through his teeth, "Little brothers, do you think he is dead now?" When he finally let go, a little bit of the widui still got him, in his face. He said, "Little brothers, I don't see you at all."

Then he told them that he was going to go and wash himself in the bay [James Bay], and after that no one would be able to drink that water. He said, "I am going to walk to the bay. The way I see it, I killed him and I'm going to be the one to give the orders. You won't have to fear the Skunk anymore, anywhere in the world." He had his head bowed down because he couldn't see.

He said, "There is not going to be another one born that size. You are going to cut him up into little pieces; throw some pieces into the woods, but throw more into the bay. (They still will fear widui, but it will not kill them anymore.) After he had given these orders he told them that he was going to go down and wash himself in the bay and after that they would not be able to drink the water from there.

And his little brothers asked him if they could go with him, but he said, "No, don't go with me." They asked, "Won't you walk into trees on the way?" He told them, "There's only going to be one tree of each kind that I'm going to walk into and then I'll come out from the bush." And he started, and walked into a tree, and asked the tree, "What kind of a tree are you ?" He walked into a pine, and a poplar, and a balsam fir, and a black spruce. And each one that he walked into talked to him. And the last one that he walked into told him that he was the only tree that stands around the bay. The last thing that he walked into was a bush, and then he walked out into the bay.

He washed himself all over, but even then he could hardly see. Then he went along the shore, looking around, and he thought about his little brothers and wondered how they were managing. He found the bones of a whale, and used one of its ribs to make himself a bow that would never break.

The Wolverine cured his eyes by the salt water. The water was not going to taste like Skunk's widui, but salty. That is why the water is salty—because of the Skunk's widui. There was a lot of water, Wolverine said, and it would be all salty.

Finally Wolverine went up inland into the bush again. His wife was dead, but he had two children. Mistabeo told him, "Someone is taking care of your children, but they are being cruel to them. Human beings have found your children, and you will see them when you find your children. The humans store up the best of everything to eat, and what is no good they give to your children. There is a small tent where your children are. I am not leaving you yet; time will come when I will leave you." After some time, Wolverine came to a camp where they were. He saw some huge tracks and thought that this was the size of the humans. He did not realize that they were wearing snowshoes.

There was nobody around when he arrived. He entered the small teepee and found his children inside. He asked them, "What do they feed you?" "We only have caribou liver," they answered.

The Wolverine went over to the human's teepee. He knew that only the human's children were there. Wolverine asked the human children, "Where are the other human beings? Why is there nobody home?" One of the children said, "They killed a lot of caribou and are getting them, bringing them in." He asked him, "Does your father have any grease?" "Yes," the child answered, "He has some outside on the cache rack." Wolverine told the child, "Let us go outside to see all of his feast."

So the child showed Wolverine, "Here it is, his grease and also the good caribou meat." Then Wolverine took all the feast food to his children's teepee, all of the food that this man was supposed to be in charge of. And he opened it and started cooking for his children. He was so angry at the humans for mistreating his children that he did this.

After he finished eating, he followed the trail of the humans who had one of the caribou. He climbed up a tree which had a big limb overhanging the trail. One of the human children had told him that his father would be back soon, bringing the best caribou meat. As the man was heading back with a toboggan loaded with meat, Wolverine watched him go underneath and then shot him in the back of the head with an arrow. He knocked the man right down. Then Wolverine pushed the body of the man off to one side of the trail and came back on the trail pulling the toboggan of caribou meat.

When the other humans came along the trail, they found their leader lying beside the trail. When they saw the track, they said, "Our brother is back." They knew that Wolverine was the one that had killed their leader. They continued to their camp and carried their caribou meat inside their teepee.

They started to discuss how they could kill Wolverine. Mistabeo told Wolverine about what they were saying. He also told him, "Stop acting and treating these people in this manner; you should not kill the humans." The people decided how they would try to kill Wolverine. "If we pass the bowl of hot caribou grease for each to take a sip, we can hit the bowl quickly as he takes his sip and the hot grease will burn his eyes." Then they started to gather the fat from their caribou.

Mistabeo told Wolverine, "They are going to invite you to their feast and they will tell you, "We are taking a sip of grease." You will be sitting near the fire. Close your eyes, but not all the way shut, and when you feel that they are trying to hit the grease pan, quickly throw it into the fire." Wolverine did this, and when he threw the grease pan into the fire, he ran out, telling them, "I have a feeling that you are trying to kill me."

The humans discussed some other way to try to kill Wolverine. They thought, "Maybe if we have a drink of hot caribou blood, that would be able to burn him. We can throw a piece of solid grease into the bowl when he is taking his drink of the hot blood." They started to prepare the feast, and one of the men was going to be ready to throw the solid grease into the big bowl while Wolverine is drinking.

But Mistabeo told Wolverine what they are going to try to do to him, and to throw it in the fire again. Then they called him, "We are eating blood. We are having a feast of blood." Wolverine commented, "My! They have a feast very often." He went in, and they told him just where to sit. He said, "What a complicated feast!" He jumped up where he was supposed to sit. They gave him the large bowl of blood. He was watching them from where he was sitting. Just as the man was about to throw the solid grease, he threw the bowl of blood into the fire. Then he jumped down and ran out. As he passed out of the door, he told them, "I still think that you are trying to kill me. Be careful of my young ones."

He left them; he went away from them because Mistabeo told him, "You will have to be by yourself and to travel alone. You will never be able to live with humans again." This is the end of the story.

A Retrospective From Grand Chief Ted Moses

The James Bay Crees or Eeyouch, as we call ourselves, have always lived on the land, which we call Eeyou Istchee or The People's Land. We were there thousands of years before Europeans came from across the sea. Yet, without the consent or even the knowledge of the Eeyouch, our land was first transferred in 1670 by quill and ink, by King Charles of England to his cousin Prince Rupert. Then in 1868, the same lands—our lands—were transferred to the Government of Canada and subsequently to Quebec in 1898. We knew nothing of any of this; we just kept on living as we always had.

When the Europeans first began to come across the ocean, we integrated fur trading into our economy and activities. Because the interest of the fur traders lay in expanding to the west up the Albany (northern Ontario) and Churchill (Manitoba) Rivers and across the Prairies, the east coast of James Bay was largely forgotten at the time. It was in the 20th century that a darker colonial agenda began to emerge.

In 1911, the National Transcontinental Railroad was built through the area just to the south of our lands. This allowed the Quebec Department of Agriculture and Colonization to extend the reach of its settlement program into the mid-North. Of course, when the farms—built on poor soils—failed the farmers turned to hunting, fishing, and trapping to survive. The newcomers were competing with Cree hunters and putting pressure on the Cree lands.

After World War I, the soldiers came back to Canada seeking work. Some of them took up contract trapping on our lands. They came in for a season and used poisoned baits and other methods to clear the land of fur-bearing animals. The Eeyouch were being pushed out of our way of life. No more could our people leave portions of our lands untrapped and unhunted in a given year. Anything left untaken would be snapped up by the contract trappers.

This challenged our traditional system of land management, based on the practice of dividing our lands into extended family hunting territories. Now, just to survive, our people had to take whatever animals they found, as did all who were hunting the land in

In the late 19th and early 20th centuries, the Quebec Department of Agriculture and Colonization, later Colonization and Mines, publicized northern agricultural opportunities. When the National Transcontinental Railroad was completed in 1913, the Abitibi area (which became part of Quebec in 1898) was opened to Euro-Canadian settlement. The marginal nature of the land and the short growing season made agriculture difficult but, beginning in the 1920s, mineral resources drew more people northward. The mines expanded in the 1930s and the provincial government renewed its colonization efforts as a way of mitigating the effects of the Great Depression. All of these factors led to the arrival of more and more Whites in the southern portions of the traditional Cree hunting areas.

competition with us. By the 1920s, many Eeyouch were afraid to go into the bush. Overharvesting had taken its toll—there was no food and a period of famine began. The Eeyouch refer to this period as "the poor times" or kachistumakich.

About this time, the Government of Quebec was beginning to feel that it had not gained adequate control of this area that had been newly appended to its north. Even though the province taxed resource extraction industries, most of the furs and lumber being harvested were slipping (by rail) into Ontario and further west, without a cent of tax going to the province from which it was being taken. Similarly, the Hudson's Bay Company was also losing control of its interests in the territory as it began to realize that its centuries of fur profits had been built on Cree land management techniques, which left enough breeding stock alive to keep the animal populations at healthy levels.

The National Transcontinental Railroad helped spur development in northern Ontario, and was used to transport northern Quebec furs and lumber to Ontario and the West, often avoiding Quebec taxation. Successive Quebec governments promoted resource extraction and the economic development of the North without regard to the claims or the interests of the Native peoples living there.

In order to deal with the crisis that was preventing our people from pursuing their traditional way of life, a project was started to manage the few remaining beaver colonies in order to re-establish the populations. A beaver preserve was opened in 1932, with the co-operation of the Province of Quebec and the federal government, and administered by the Hudson's Bay Company. The Eeyouch conducted annual surveys of the beaver colonies and the Government of Quebec agreed to close the area to non-Cree hunters and trappers. After eight years, the Crees began to harvest the beavers, respecting quotas. The program of quotas was based on the ancient and sophisticated Cree way of managing the resources. It was still going on in our lands into the 1970s. In fact, it still runs today in a similar manner. The program was promoted by the federal government and caught fire not only in Eeyou Istchee, but indeed right across Canada.

From Trading Post to Town

By the 1950s and 1960s, the Hudson's Bay Company trading posts began to transform into towns that were a collection of houses, shacks, and tent frames. A growing number of education and health workers had begun to come up from the south. With the old-age pension (a federal benefit given to the aged) being introduced in the 1950s, elders with health problems began to stay in towns rather than going into the bush with their families.

These new towns had problems. The growing number of Cree residences occupied year-round in these communities were not supported by any infrastructure. There was no source of drinking water for the people, other than a tap at the back of the school or the teacher's house, or a hole in the river ice. There were no sanitary services other than outhouses and ditches. In Eastmain, where I am from, we had only one radiophone connecting us to the outside world. This was how it was in the communities in the 1960s and early 1970s.

As their name implies, residential schools were governmentally sanctioned institutions that housed and schooled children who had been removed from the influences of traditional Cree family life.

There were federally administered day schools operating at Chisasibi by 1910, at Mistissini and Waswanipi by 1914, and at Eastmain by 1939. In addition, there were Anglican and Roman Catholic residential schools at Chisasibi by 1922 and 1936, respectively.

Both residential and day schools—through their curriculums and, in the case of the former, the isolation they imposed on Native students—encouraged assimilation into the Euro-Canadian culture. They also discouraged the transmission of Native traditions, customs, and languages.

Following World War II, the federal government took a completely different approach and encouraged the integration of Native students into provincial education systems. Day schools and residential schools were still being opened in the early 1960s.

The Legacy of the Canadian School System

The 20th century also brought residential schools for the Crees. Earlier, in the 19th century, Methodist missionaries and then the Anglican Church had organized summer day schools in Cree communities. These schools had accommodated the Cree way of life by being organized in the season when groups of people came together in summer camps.

With the advent of residential schools, Cree families would leave their children in the residences and then go into the bush for the fall and winter, or education officials would visit bush camps in planes, and children would be flown out to the schools. In the 1960s, day schools began to operate year-round for the lower grades. Because of this, it became necessary for children to stay in town, often with their mothers or with other relatives, while the men hunted in the bush.

Residential schools took students just to the end of junior grade school (Grade 8). For years, this was the end of schooling for most Cree students. Throughout their schooling years, young Crees were segregated from their own community while they were in residence, but they lived within Cree communities. The families would be visible to them and the odd time they would be allowed to eat the traditional Cree foods on which they had grown up.

Aside from the fact that the curriculum was based on a program of assimilation, there was abuse (physical, emotional, sexual), although it was perhaps less prevalent in the James Bay schools than it was elsewhere in Canada. Another aspect of the tragedy of these schools was the loss of life due to tuberculosis. The registers from the schools contain page after page of accounts of students who died while their parents were in the bush.

Because many of our young people did not go into the bush with their families, the residential school legacy in the communities caused a generation of students to miss the training of growing up as Eeyouch. In our culture, we have subtle ways of teaching. We encourage individuals to become independent and to believe that the skills they possess are due to their own efforts. The students who came back from the schools did not have the traditional skills an Eeyou person their age would normally have. For many, the opportunity to learn Eeyou skills and knowledge was no longer there, or at least not easy to obtain when they returned, because their parents were ill or family circumstances had changed. Today, many Eeyou in their forties and fifties feel this lack of real education and nurturing in their childhood upbringing.

A New Generation of Crees

However awful the legacy of the residential schools, they did open up the communities to outside realities. With Cree children who spoke English or French, the Eeyouch were no longer dependent upon the church ministers or the Hudson's Bay Company employees for their relations with the governments. As the complexity of Eeyouch–government relations increased in the 1970s, those sons and daughters of the hunting families who were educated in the residential schools assumed key roles—as chiefs, health workers, and owners of businesses.

In the early 1970s, a number of us finished high school in the south and came home to our communities. We were the first generation to finish high school in any numbers. At the time, some of the chiefs, in particular Robert Kanatewat, were beginning to go to the meetings of the Indians of Quebec Association. There was a growing sense that our rights to the land and our unity as the Eeyouch were important to the future of our communities.

The Indians of Quebec Association, established in 1966, formed part of a continent-wide movement to provide Native peoples with a political and lobbying voice. Although each Cree community had a chief at that time, and the Crees felt they had political unity, they did not have a recognized political organization. In 1971, the Crees turned to this association to help them press their claims against the Province of Quebec and its plans to develop the James Bay hydroelectric power project.

As a first step, our leadership sought to have the federal Department of Indian Affairs and Northern Development programs apply to our communities. We obviously needed housing, jobs, and better health services. We also needed recognition of our rights, as mining and forestry were starting to destroy the lands of many of the families living in the bush.

Then on April 30, 1971, we were stunned to hear a radio announcement that the Province of Quebec was planning to build three hydroelectric complexes on our lands in James Bay. We were not given any advanced warning of the proposal. Sure, we had picked up the possibility that something was coming, as we had seen the exploration crews for a few years. But Premier Robert Bourassa's public announcement of the project of the century was made as though we did not exist, had never existed.

Hydroelectric Development for Eeyou Istchee

The post-World War II boom fueled development of mining and forestry enterprises, which had been moving northward since before World War I. To complement this resource development, Premier Robert Bourassa announced the James Bay Project in 1971. The plan was to generate hydroelectricity by diverting the waters of Eastmain, Opinaca, and Caniapiscau Rivers to the La Grande River. The La Grande River was Quebec's third largest and the largest river flowing into James Bay. It was to become a vast reservoir and the location for the world's largest underground powerhouse.

The diversion would flood 10,500 square kilometres (4054 square miles) of prime Cree hunting land. The same year, the Quebec government created the James Bay Development Corporation to oversee the project and began to build roads, airports, and construction sites in Cree territory.

The first phase of the James Bay Project is referred to as James I or the La Grande Project. A second phase was planned, to begin in 1989. It is identified as James II or the Great Whale Project, after the northern river at its centre. The plan for this phase called for the development of generators along the Great Whale River, to the north of the La Grande River, and the Nottaway, Broadback, and Rupert Rivers to the south.

Billy Diamond was the first Grand Chief of the Grand Council of the Crees. He played a central role in the negotiations leading up to the James Bay and Northern Quebec Agreement of 1975.

Philip Awashish was among the first of his generation of Cree people to attend university. He became embroiled in the James Bay Project controversy and used his skills and knowledge to present the Crees' arguments against the power project.

We believed our lands were being stolen. Billy Diamond and Philip Awashish were the first to raise the alarm, and we began to organize ourselves to counter this threat. We had seen the workers come into our towns "looking for a little fun," and disrupting the communities. So our immediate concern was to secure our towns from intruders. We negotiated an agreement with the James Bay Energy Corporation (the separate corporation responsible for the construction of dams, generators, and related infrastructure) that their workers could not come into our communities without permission. We then mounted our first opposition through the Indians of Quebec Association.

Our concerns were immediate: stop the project, get recognition of our rights, and take control of the government services in our communities. We then decided that we needed a Cree voice to fight for our rights. We formed the Notchimeeweeyouch, Winnigegoweeyouch Enatimadouch, which means "Inlanders and Coasters Working for Their Mutual Benefit." In English, it was the Grand Council of the Crees and in French, Le Grand Conseil des Cris. A Grand Chief was elected for the council through a democratic, popular election.

We filed a court case based on our rights to our homeland. We also filed for an injunction to stop the ongoing damages caused by the construction of the La Grande Project. In November 1973, after the longest interlocutory injunction hearing in Canadian history, Mr. Justice Albert Malouf of the Quebec Superior Court granted a court order to stop the construction. One week later, the Quebec Court of Appeal overturned this decision, stating that it was in the interest of Quebec's population for the project to continue and that the damage to Cree rights, if any, could be compensated.

This was a severe blow. Our faith in the Canadian legal system had been shaken. But, apparently Hydro-Québec and the Government of Quebec had also been shaken by the prospect that the Crees, a long disregarded people, might have rights to the land—rights that were competitive with their claims. An offer to negotiate came within a week of the ruling by the Quebec Court of Appeal. We had to weigh whether we would survive as a people until we won on the basis of the merits of the main case in the lower court, and finally in the Supreme Court of Canada. We had to decide if the impacts of the damages to the land and to the people would be too much for the people to survive.

The question for us to consider was whether a system that forced us, the underdog in this affair, to fight for our rights (while our lands and way of life were being destroyed and we were being told we were squatters) would be likely to uphold our rights. Or, as already had been done, would this system twist them so that we would lose. If we did lose, we recognized that we would lose any leverage that we might otherwise have in discussions with the Province of Quebec and the Government of Canada to resolve issues in a treaty. In either case, we knew that the La Grande River was lost and that it would take years for us to get final justice.

We had communities to build and people to care for, so we decided to negotiate. It took until November 1974 to complete the Agreement in Principle for a treaty between the Crees (and Inuit), the two levels of government, and the corporate parties involved in the James Bay Project. The Agreement in Principle set out the subject matters to be negotiated, and then we set a one-year deadline for completion of the discussions. Approximately one year later, in November 1975, the Crees and the Inuit of Northern Quebec signed the James Bay and Northern Quebec Agreement (often referred to as a treaty) with the Province of Quebec, the Government of Canada, Hydro-Québec, the James Bay Development Corporation, and the James Bay Energy Corporation. The Agreement set out a payment of approximately $125 million to the Crees and $100 million to the Inuit in compensation.

The principle behind the Agreement, as expressed by then Member of the National Assembly and former Quebec representative in the negotiations John Ciaccia, in his speech to the National Assembly when he presented the Agreement for approval, is to provide a choice. He stated: "Finally, and perhaps most important, the Native peoples are offered a choice. They will be free, as individuals, to choose between their traditional occupations and new occupations."

We would be free to continue our traditional ways on the land or to seek participation in the Quebec economy through employment and entrepreneurial opportunities. The Agreement was set up to bring about Cree and Inuit participation in the development of the James Bay territory, as defined in the Agreement, and to regulate this development so that our way of life on the land would still be a viable alternative. This required strict social and environmental rules, as outlined in the Agreement as "the environmental and social protection regime for the Territory," and a regulatory regime to respond to the

To the north of the Cree, the Inuit people and their lands would also be affected by the James Bay hydroelectric project.

The parties to the James Bay and Northern Quebec Agreement included the Grand Council of the Crees and the Northern Quebec Inuit Association. In 1978, the Naskapi of Schefferville (on the border with Labrador) negotiated the Northern Quebec Agreement. It was modelled on the 1975 Agreement and brought the Naskapi into the same relationship with the governments of Canada and Quebec as the Crees and Inuit agreed to in 1975.

It wasn't until 1984 that the Cree-Naskapi Act of Quebec resulted from the 1975 Agreement and related agreements. Hailed as the first self-government legislation for Aboriginal people in Canada, it replaced the Indian Act for the regions it serves and established the communities as corporate entities. Its legal priority is second to that of the James Bay and Northern Quebec Native Claims Settlement Act (1977), the federal statute that gave effect to the James Bay and Northern Quebec Agreement.

peculiarities of our situation. Of the Cree way of life and these rules Mr. Ciaccia went on to state:

> *So we are by no means talking about a dying way of life. On the contrary, it is strongly maintained. The Native peoples hold to it with every fibre of their being. And as the North is inevitably opened up to other peoples, it would be wrong not to do what is in our power to do to guarantee and protect this way of life.*
>
> *We are naturally much worried about the preservation of the environment. This question has indeed been one of our main preoccupations. That is why there will be a specific Environmental and Social Regime in the North. Its guiding principle will be development in harmony with the protecting of the environment.*
>
> *As I have said, and I will no doubt often say it again: there is no question of stopping development. But there will be procedure to study the possible effects of specific development projects and to determine how these effects, where they may be detrimental, can be prevented or minimized. And this will not be a unilateral action. The Native peoples will have a part in deciding and establishing environmental regulations that directly affect them and their way of life.*

The 1975 Agreement is like the Nunavut Agreement and the Gitxsan Treaty rolled into one. It contains a total of 30 sections that deal with Cree and Inuit matters. It has common sections on Principal Provisions; Eligibility; Preliminary Territorial Descriptions; Technical Aspects (primarily on the La Grande Project); Hunting, Fishing and Trapping; and Compensation and Taxation.

Nunavut Agreement and Gitxsan Treaty

The Nunavut Land Settlement Agreement of 1993 led eventually to the creation of Nunavut as a new territory, covering about one-sixth of Canada's land mass. Through this Agreement, the region's 17,500 Inuit received compensation, and retained hunting and trapping rights as well as ownership of 350,000 square kilometres (135,146 square miles) of the land. Nunavut now has a Legislative Assembly and powers equivalent to other federal territories.

In 1984, the Gitxsan and Wet'swwet'en peoples commenced a court action claiming ownership and jurisdiction over 58,000 square kilometres (22,396 square miles) of land in northern British Columbia (B.C.). Although the B.C. Supreme Court ruled against the Native claims, a B.C. Court of Appeal ruling in 1993 upheld the concept of Aboriginal rights. A Supreme Court of Canada decision in 1997 recognized Aboriginal rights without addressing the Gitxsan question specifically, and recommended the parties return to negotiations to settle their outstanding land title issues. In 1998, a Reconciliation Agreement issued by the Supreme Court set the stage for renewed Gitxsan–provincial government negotiations over land title, government administration, and other matters of common concern.

It then has separate Cree and Inuit sections on Land Selection, Land Regime, Local Government, Regional Government, Health and Social Services, Education, Police, Administration of Justice, Environment and Future Development, and Economic and Social Development. It also has provisions for an Income Security Program for Cree Hunters and Trappers.

The Income Security Program for Cree hunters and trappers was set up in 1976 with the primary objective of encouraging the continuation and survival of a traditional way of life by, among other things, providing Cree hunters and trappers with a guaranteed income. The program is intended for Crees residing in Quebec who carry out wildlife harvesting activities as a way of life.

Many saw the Agreement as a panacea. Premier Bourassa spoke out in favour of it, as did then Prime Minister Pierre Elliott Trudeau. Opposition parties disparaged it; Joe Clark, leader of the Progressive Conservative Party, stood up in the House of Commons and derided it because it had been negotiated under duress. He was absolutely right. As Billy Diamond said, we were negotiating with a gun to our heads. At the time, we saw it as our only hope as the project was going ahead, with or without our input. It was clear to us that, if we were not able to come to some agreement with the governments and corporations, we would not have the means to build our communities and it would be difficult for us to protect our rights against further incursions.

After the Agreement was signed, we went to the Cree communities to have it ratified by the people. We had to fly around to all of the communities to explain the Agreement. We also had to set up a process whereby everyone would have the possibility of voting. We had three months for this.

Many of us saw the Agreement as having failed in many respects. What it contained was recognition of some Cree rights, but people saw that the governments of Quebec and Canada were reluctant to really accept the existence of a Cree Government. This fact is reflected in the absence of the English or French words for "Cree Government" from the Agreement. A year or so after the Agreement was signed, the province wanted to affirm the regulatory regime for Cree governance. The Cree Regional Authority was the name that had been agreed to at the table during the Agreement negotiations. However, the provincial negotiators wanted to record the name of the institution in the provincial legislation not just in French and English, but also in Cree. We searched for an expression, but the only one that we could come up with was "Eeyou Tabeytachesiw" or Cree Government, just as Quebec Tabeytachesiw and Canada Tabeytachesiw means the Government of Quebec and the Government of Canada. This is what the provincial legislation states today: Eeyou Tabeytachesiw!

In most of our sessions with our people, it was evident that they saw the Agreement as having severe flaws. However, the people also saw that the Agreement represented a chance to make progress and that it was but the first acknowledgement by the governments of Canada and Quebec of at least some Cree rights.

What many Aboriginal people saw as the primary fault in the Agreement was our acceptance that some of the institutions of Cree Government would be set up under Quebec law. The Cree School Board, the Cree Board of Health and Social Services, and the Cree Regional Authority, as well as part of the Cree governance of community lands; the Income Security Program for Cree hunters and trappers; policing and justice; social and environmental protection; and the hunting, fishing, and trapping regime all fall under the jurisdiction of the province as do matters relating to future development, community, and economic development.

Acceptance of provincial involvement in these areas was thought of as a denial of the nation-to-nation status of Aboriginal dealings with the Government of Canada. First of all, we thought that in the past the federal government had served us poorly in many of these areas. Second, we thought that the Crees would have more input into the evolution of these systems of governance if we were not under one level of government. Finally, we believed that the federal government, as the senior level of government in this arrangement, would not be out of the picture in case the province failed in its treaty obligations to us.

At the time, Canadians saw the Agreement as the best way of working with Aboriginal people, to provide a future for them. Today, in much the same way, the Nunavut Agreement is seen as the best solution. The Crees were setting up regulatory regimes that accommodated, to some extent, the evolution of Canadian public government. The Northern Quebec Inuit went even further in the Agreement in this regard. They accepted that non-Inuit residents of their communities could run for and hold public office in the governance of the territory. Essentially, the Inuit saw this as a gamble. To get powers of administration over the whole of the territory under one governmental regime, the Inuit bet that they would always be the majority of the population in their part of the territory and that, in spite of their openness to non-Aboriginal involvement, Inuit would maintain control.

To the Crees, such a regime would not have gone far enough in protecting Cree interests. There were non-Cree towns, built around resource extraction, already established in the southern part of our lands. Moreover, the Province of Quebec had already set up agencies and instruments of public governance in the south, such as the James Bay Energy Corporation and the James Bay Development Corporation. The province had expressed its unwillingness to dissolve these, so we opted for regimes that would give us strong participation in the control of these agencies.

In spite of all these concerns, however, the Crees did ratify the Agreement. Although a minority of the eligible Cree voters ratified it, of the 24 percent that did vote, only one person voted against it. On this basis, we went forward.

It took two years for the governments of Canada and Quebec to ratify the Agreement in legislation. Quebec legislated the environment regime, Cree local government on Category IB lands, the Cree Regional Authority, the Cree School Board, and the Cree Board of Health and Social Services. The federal government made commitments in the Agreement to legislate a social and environmental protection regime and, if necessary, to implement this regulatory regime. Since that time, and in spite of its inability to deliver the promised regime, the federal government has insisted that further legislation beyond its James Bay and Northern Quebec Native Claims Settlement Act of 1976–77 is unnecessary to implement the Agreement. This is ironic, as I will discuss presently.

We were perhaps wrong to be optimistic when the Agreement was signed in November 1975. However, the promise that we had been waiting for had been made, and the intricacies of implementation had not yet become an obstacle. The difficulties began shortly after the Agreement was confirmed by the federal and provincial governments, and by the Crees and Inuit. Almost nothing happened. Neither the Canadian nor the Quebec government had made any plans for implementation. When we convened a meeting

The 1975 Agreement sets out Cree rights to continue their traditional way of life over the whole of the territory and also to become involved in development. This right is to be given priority when considering development projects, awarding jobs and contracts, approving the outfitting camps, and regulating sport hunting and fishing. Cree representatives sit on committees with Quebec and Canada that are to recommend legislation and regulations to protect these rights. The Agreement also states that Crees are to be employed in the policing and enforcement of game laws in the territory.

According to the Agreement, all lands were transferred to the Province of Quebec and, in the case of Category 1A lands, their administration was transferred back to Canada to be held as lands set aside for the Crees. In addition to the 1A lands, there are 1B and 1B special lands that are under Cree local government jurisdiction.

On Category 1 lands the Crees control access for purposes of development and in this way control the extraction of minerals, although the sub-surface belongs nominally to Quebec. Over the 5,542 square kilometres (2,140 square miles) of Category 1 lands the Crees have the exclusive right to hunt, fish, and trap and to the commercial development of the resources.

On Category 2 lands, 62,155 square kilometres (24,000 square miles), the Crees have the exclusive right to hunt, fish, and trap and have a right to replacement or compensation for land expropriated for public purposes. This land is administered by a Regional Zone Council on which the Crees appoint three members and the James Bay Municipality appoints three members.

On Category 3 lands (the rest of the territory), administered by the James Bay Municipality and the Province of Quebec, the Crees have the exclusive right to certain species of fish and animals and the priorities and protections described above as administered by the joint Cree–Quebec committees set up for this purpose.

of the Joint Economic and Community Development Committee, the federal government representatives at the meeting said that they did not have a mandate but were there only as observers. Similarly, the representatives for the Province of Quebec were uncertain about their mandate. At the second meeting, they stated that they could no longer participate because the new separatist government refused to allow meetings between federal and provincial officials without special approval.

The 1975 Agreement established the Joint Economic and Community Development Committee to provide a vehicle for the Cree people and the two levels of government to review and make recommendations respecting the establishment, expansion, operation, and effectiveness of government programs related to the economic and social development of the Cree people. The Committee was composed of nine members: two from the Government of Canada, two from the Province of Quebec, and five appointed by the Cree Regional Authority.

At the time that the James Bay and Northern Quebec Agreement was signed, our only power was the unity expressed in the Grand Council of the Crees, which had only recently been formed. Cree communities—and indeed Cree local governance—were in disarray. In Cree villages, people hauled water using a yoke or, if they were lucky, a snowmobile and a 200-litre (45-gallon) drum. Sanitation facilities were outhouses, which were often built on saturated clays with little capacity to absorb water. Half of the population, when they were in town, lived in wooden-sided tents (some lived year-round in these) or in dilapidated and overcrowded houses. Very few Crees had electricity in their dwellings. The communities did not have proper roads, and in the rainy season the laneways would flood out and the communities would turn into seas of sewage-reeking mud. The communities had minimal funding to build and support community services. The schools and health clinics were in poor condition and ill-equipped.

In health services, as in education, being wards of the Crown meant that the local people did not have input into the types of services that were provided. The services had been determined without reference to the needs and, as a result, things were out of control. The communities suffered a human cost for the way things were being run. This is one of the things that we attempted to correct with the Agreement.

After the Agreement was confirmed in legislation, the environmental committees began to meet. However, the budgets set aside for this were not sufficient to staff them properly or to carry out the mandates of the regulatory regimes. The federal government set up a northern Quebec office for environmental and social protection, but it closed the office two years later, in 1980, without apparent reason. To us, the priority and the budgets seemed to be going toward cleaning up the St. Lawrence!

In the Cree communities, the situation continued to deteriorate. Without adequate drinking water and sewage disposal facilities, disease began to break out. Gastroenteritis swept through the communities in the late 1970s and early 1980s. The Crees began spending their own compensation funds to build sewage systems as Canada and Quebec refused to meet their treaty obligations in this regard. In communities like Waskaganish, the Department of Indian Affairs and Northern Development had dug six-metre (20-foot) ditches around the community to drain the site, but these were left there for years. The surface run-off just mixed with sewage, forming large pools around the houses.

The Grand Chief at the time, Billy Diamond, took the matter to the Standing Committee of Parliament on Aboriginal Affairs and to the ministers of Justice, Indian Affairs and Northern Development, and Health. Finally, in 1981, an extensive federal review of the implementation of the James Bay and Northern Quebec Agreement was conducted. The review was undertaken by the late John Tait, Assistant Deputy Minister of the Department of Indian Affairs and Northern Development, and the results were published in a report in 1982. It confirmed much of what the Crees, Inuit, and Naskapis had stated.

Once the deplorable health conditions were confirmed, a modest action plan was put into place to resolve some of the immediate problems. The health clinics in the communities were renovated. In addition, the Government of Canada accepted the fact that sewer and water systems were needed, and it reimbursed the Crees for any monies already spent in this regard. The review also resulted in the immediate initiation of discussions on the legislation for setting up the local community governments, which had been promised in the treaty. These discussions were finalized in 1984 and the Cree-Naskapi (of Quebec) Act was passed by Parliament in the same year.

While the Government of Canada, in co-operation with the Crees and Inuit, conducted a review of its performance in implementing the Agreement, the Government of Quebec underfunded the school board and health and social services board. In 1978, the provincial government sent a letter to the Crees stating that the programs for community development did not apply to their communities because the Crees had opted for federal lands in the Agreement. Despite the many clauses that require Quebec's participation, Quebec unilaterally abrogated the treaty when it refused to implement clauses such as the following:

The term "wards of the Crown" comes from the policy of guardianship developed by colonial and federal departments of Indian affairs in their dealings with Native peoples. In essence, the federal government treated Native peoples as wards who needed to be protected from the worst elements of White culture and society while, at the same time, being groomed as productive members of that society. The tangible results of this authoritarian and assimilationist policy were reserves, Indian agents, and a government bureaucracy that administered to the needs of its charges without much input from them or attention to their perceptions of their own best interests and goals.

In the 1970s and 1980s, provincial and federal governments began to pay more attention to pollution issues—smog, acid rain, mercury poisoning, ozone depletion, water and air contaminants, pesticides and chemicals in the environment. In the 1980s the federal government's Department of the Environment embarked upon an ambitious program to clean up the Great Lakes and the St. Lawrence Waterway.

28.11.1.... Quebec and Canada shall provide funding and technical assistance for:

a) the construction or provision of a community centre in each Cree community;

b) essential sanitation services in each Cree community;

c) fire protection including the training of Crees, the purchase of equipment and, when necessary, the construction of facilities in each Cree community.

As a result of the provincial government's and federal government's lack of attention to their obligations to the Crees, we realized that treaties between the federal government and Aboriginal peoples were in fact entered into as not much more than a ruse to clear the Canadian government's access to the lands and resources of Aboriginal peoples. We had entered into the 1975 Agreement with a commitment to develop the territory co-operatively. We realized that this was not the intention of either the federal or provincial government. The program became one of pushing the Crees out of the process of developing the territory and of doing as little as possible about the development of the Cree communities.

International Action

In 1978–79, we were shocked by the realization that neither the Canadian nor the Quebec government had taken its commitments to the Cree people seriously. It seemed as if they had signed the treaty to get what they wanted and had planned to use every manner of subterfuge possible to avoid having to provide the promised services and programs to the Crees. The rights and services accorded to the Crees in the 1975 Agreement were apparently seen as things to be minimized, eroded, and denied in the future.

Seeing this dishonesty on the part of the governments of Canada and Quebec, we decided that we would seek international involvement in the implementation of the treaty. It seemed to us that the implementation of treaties between countries was much more a matter of international concern and a matter of pride within Canada than was the fulfillment of treaties to Aboriginal peoples within Canada. We thought that it was necessary to bring the issue to the international arena and, by doing so, to bring it to the attention of the Canadian public.

We therefore decided to ask for an audience with Pope John Paul II because few in the international community could speak with such moral authority. The strategy worked. In the newspaper *Le Devoir*, after we returned from Italy, there was a political cartoon on the upcoming visit by Premier René Lévesque to the Pope. In the cartoon, the Pope is receiving Premier Levesque and he is leaning over to him and asking: "You're from Quebec. Do you know Billy Diamond?"

Left to right: Pope John Paul II, Ted Moses, Philip Awashish, Billy Diamond.

In the early 1980s, we began our efforts to work with the United Nations (UN) on Aboriginal rights. The Supreme Court of Canada had just upheld the discriminatory provisions of the Indian Act. The case that had been appealed to the Supreme Court involved the article of the Indian Act that barred Aboriginal women who married non-Aboriginal men, and their children, from being registered as Indians under the Act. However, the Act allowed for non-Aboriginal women who married Aboriginal men, and their children, to be registered. It was a clear case of sexual discrimination within an Act, which was a racist piece of legislation in itself, to regulate the affairs of Aboriginal peoples. We appealed this decision to the UN Human Rights Committee. This appeal, as well as the efforts of the Crees, opened the eyes of many in the UN community to the fact that discrimination continued in the internal affairs of large countries like Canada.

On another level of international action, we participated in the International Labour Office's drafting of its revision of Convention 107, the Indigenous and Tribal Populations Convention, 1957, which resulted in Convention 169, the Convention Concerning Indigenous and Tribal Peoples in Independent Countries, 1989. This exercise gave us contacts within governments around the world and within the governments of Indigenous peoples. It helped us to better understand the need for international standards for the treatment of these peoples.

To get standing at the UN, we applied for and got recognition as a "non- governmental organization" that could advise the UN on its efforts to formulate policies and laws for Indigenous peoples. This resulted in the Draft Declaration on the Rights of Indigenous Peoples in 1993 and has recently led to the creation of a Permanent Forum for Indigenous Issues at the UN. It also resulted in the declaration of an International Decade of the World's Indigenous People (1995–2005).

The kinds of things that we had to fight for convinced us more than ever about the importance of this work. We had to fight to be recognized as "peoples," with an "s." In international law, peoples have fundamental collective rights to self-determination, to continue to use their natural wealth and resources to maintain and develop their communities, and most of all to never, jamais, weeskat, be deprived of their own means of subsistence. Note that the International Decade mentioned above has only the singular word "people" in its title. This is because many countries opposed this status of "peoples" for Aboriginal peoples, as they did not want this right to self-determination and to lands, natural wealth, and resources to be recognized as applying to them.

For years, we fought for the "s." We got it in the text of the Draft Declaration, but missed having it used in some of the other UN initiatives.

We have also fought for the treaties between the Government of Canada and Aboriginal peoples in Canada to be recognized as treaties under international law. We fought for this because we noticed that Canada and many other countries used higher standards in the implementation of their international treaties than they used in regard to their infamous broken treaties with Aboriginal peoples. We wanted also to have recourse to international courts to adjudicate issues that might not be deemed to be discriminatory in Canada, such as the case on the Indian status of Aboriginal women who married non-Aboriginal men.

This is what we were and still are trying to do: we are trying to obtain respect for our status and rights, and to make the James Bay and Northern Quebec Agreement work as it was intended to do. We are aiming for full protection and promotion of our language and way of life, and for equity in employment participation and in living standards. We have not yet succeeded, and we have a long way to go.

In 1984, the federal government opened the James Bay and Northern Quebec and Northeastern Quebec Claims Implementation Office. This was an attempt to fix one of the major problems pointed out by the Tait report on the implementation of the James Bay and Northern Quebec Agreement: the lack of federal government policy, plans, and machinery for the implementation of the 1975 Agreement. We began to make some progress. While the new office did not have a budget or strong mandate, it did manage to implement the 1984 Cree-Naskapi (of Quebec) Act concerning local government, and it facilitated funding subsidies for the local government operations of the eight Cree communities recognized at that time. The Act, called for in the 1975 and 1978 Agreements, incorporated the communities under federal law and set out a regime for local governance consistent with the provisions of the 1975 Agreement. At this time, many of the Crees who had led the fight against the La Grande Project, and been embroiled in subsequent negotiations, went home to become chiefs. They were needed there to set up the local governments.

The Claims Implementation Office facilitated a system of funding for the local governments that is still in place today whereby communities receive grant funding for both capital and operational needs. Spending is reported annually to the Canadian government. The local administration's major decisions are subject to local referendums to make the councils more accountable to their electorate. After 16 years, the Act now needs to be amended to recognize the Cree Nation Government and its powers, but it has served better than the Indian Act that applies elsewhere.

When the Progressive Conservatives came to power in 1985, they dismantled the Claims Implementation Office, and they turned the process of negotiating with the Crees over to one of the party faithful from Toronto. His stated goal was to cap the 1975 Agreement by arranging for a buy-out of any Cree rights that remained outstanding. Moreover, the Conservatives failed to set up the funding formulas for local government that were called for when the Cree/Naskapi Act was passed. These formulas were intended to adjust the funding to take account of the changing realities in the communities. (When the Liberal Party came to power in 1993, they created a new Claims Implementation Office.)

In addition to this, the Conservative government did an about-face on the Crees. One of the Cree communities, Oujé-Bougoumou, had been left out of the 1975 Agreement, although commitments had been made at the time to include them at a later date. This had not yet happened, so the members of that community—having been evicted from two of their former community sites by a mining development and then by the federal government—were living in plywood shacks along the side of the roads in the Chibougamau area. Prime Minister Brian Mulroney wrote to the Grand Council of the Crees on this subject and stated that the issue would be dealt with in a satisfactory manner. On the advice of the Department of Indian Affairs and Northern Development, he then did nothing. Around 1987, when we asked for discussions on this subject, he consulted with the Department of Justice, and then appointed his Toronto negotiator to settle the issue.

Let me just say that negotiations were slow and the Crees had to resort to a road-block at one point to bring attention to the issue. Eventually, with the active involvement of the Province of Quebec, the creation of the new community of Oujé-Bougoumou was agreed to.

We refused to negotiate on the treaty with the Toronto representative, unless the outstanding issues of Oujé-Bougoumou and the local government funding were settled and his mandate was changed by Cabinet to one of implementing, not extinguishing, the treaty. We eventually settled the issue of the local government funding, but the issue of Oujé-Bougoumou took another year—until 1989—to resolve. Recognition of Oujé-Bougoumou has not yet been included in amendments to the 1975 Agreement or the Cree-Naskapi Act. The treaty implementation has never been resolved either.

In 1985, Hydro-Québec decided that it would change the configuration of the La Grande Project and asked the Crees for permission to change the technical description of the project contained in the Agreement. We reviewed the request and decided that this might be an opportunity to get Hydro-Québec to commit to hiring some Crees into permanent jobs on the project. We also hoped to get Hydro-Québec and the province to set up some remedial measures to deal with the mercury contamination of the fish in the reservoirs.

The cause for the mercury contamination of fish in the reservoirs was found to be the decomposition of trees as a result of the flooding. The Cree Regional Authority's 1996 annual report stated that the mercury levels in the fish found in the La Grande Project reservoirs had apparently stabilized by 1994. The levels of contamination seemed, at that point, to be approaching those found elsewhere in the James Bay territory, although there was variation among reservoirs as well as among species of fish.

In 1986, a Mercury Agreement was signed by the Grand Council of the Crees, Hydro-Québec, and the Government of Quebec whereby a process was set up to study the impacts of contamination and to help the Crees access uncontaminated fish outside the reservoirs. In the same year, the Grand Council of the Crees, Hydro-Québec and the James Bay Energy Corporation signed the La Grande Agreement whereby the Crees were paid compensation of $110 million for increased damages above and beyond what had been stipulated in the 1975 Agreement. In addition, Hydro-Québec and the Crees set a target period of 10 years for 150 Crees to be trained and hired to work on the operations of the La Grande Project.

Hydro-Québec's approach to meeting its commitment to hire Crees was to take a former construction camp that they were going to dismantle and to turn it into a school for training Crees. This school was mainly for teaching heavy equipment driving skills, and we wondered how 150 heavy equipment drivers would be used on a completed project. Of the 25 or so who received training at the site, Hydro-Québec eventually hired only about five. The others were put on a waiting list to be hired later. None were subsequently called up. Moreover, we noticed that the funding for other types of employment training that had been coming from the Canadian government were cut during that time. We found out that Hydro-Québec had applied and received this funding to run their program. When we complained that the Canadian government was paying for Hydro-Québec's commitments with funds earmarked for the Crees, the funding was redirected back to the training programs in the communities. Hydro-Québec closed the school.

What we could not figure out was why the approach to the commitment to create 150 jobs for Crees was not based on a wider strategy. Could we not develop a Hydro-Québec liaison at the Cree School Board and develop summer student programs and career counselling programs? How would we deal with the union issues and also the commitment in the 1975 treaty to allow Crees access to jobs even when they did not meet French language requirements? (Hydro-Québec's collective agreement with its employees stated that employees with seniority had priority over all others, including the Crees. As well, the working environment at Hydro-Québec was French and, at the time, very few Crees spoke French.) Instead of these approaches, the Crees were offered heavy equipment jobs or nothing. It was an initiative destined to fail.

By the end of the 1980s, many of the Cree communities had been relocated and reorganized, but there were major community development and treaty issues left

Matthew Coon Come was born on his father's trapline in the James Bay Cree territory in 1956. He studied Political Science at Trent University and was a twice elected band chief. In 1987, he became Grand Chief of the Grand Council of the Crees and led the successful public campaign against the Great Whale Project. He went on to lead Cree opposition to Premier Jacques Parizeau's effort to separate Quebec from Canada, which culminated in separate provincial and Cree referendums in October 1995. In 2000, he was elected National Chief of the Assembly of First Nations and remains a powerful force in Canadian politics.

unresolved. The communities were short of meeting national housing standards by more than 700 living units, an outrageous number. Police and fire protection services were minimal, and community sewer and water services were still well behind community needs. The unemployment rate was 40 percent, with 200 to 300 young Crees entering the labour market each year. Almost nobody from the Cree communities worked in the vibrant resource development sector that immediately surrounded these communities. This was seen by our people—who were ready, willing, and able to be trained and included—as simply race-based exclusion.

As if this was not enough for us to cope with, it was in this context that Quebec announced in 1989 that it would go ahead with Phase II of the James Bay Project. It would start with the Great Whale Project and later go ahead with the Nottaway, Broadback, and Rupert's Project. Premier Robert Bourassa's plan was to sell the electricity to the United States, and they were close to finalizing agreements. As he had explained to Quebecers many times during his campaign to stay in power, the population of Quebec was decreasing while electricity demand in the United States was increasing. By selling this power to Americans, Quebec would become the Saudi Arabia of electricity.

The Crees met in March 1989 in a General Assembly. We held meetings to review the nature of the proposed projects: how much land would be flooded, damages to Cree hunting lands, the ecological and social impacts in light of the La Grande experience, possible employment and monetary benefits (the Province of Quebec had made a preliminary offer of $110 million just to get discussions going), and impacts on Cree rights. For our plenary session, which lasted two days, we conducted the discussions without the benefit of professional advice. This was to be a debate of the heart. At the end of it, the decision of the Assembly was to oppose the project in order to stop it.

The Grand Council chiefs held a strategy session afterwards, and it was decided that the courts and a public strategy would be used to bring the issue to the world audience. Our work at the international level on rights had made the Cree people very aware of the potential that lay in applying international standards to such a proposal.

The fight against the Great Whale Project and the Nottaway, Broadback, and Rupert's Project could be the subject of an epic book in itself: a small, isolated group of Indigenous people took on the government of a large province in a G-8 country, and one of the largest hydroelectric energy corporations in the world, and won. Grand Chief Matthew Coon Come really took the message to the world. To save the rivers, the Crees from the communities and the Grand Chief went to Vermont, New York, Washington (D.C.), Massachusetts, and New Hampshire; to Spain, Holland, Germany, Norway, Australia, Russia, Brazil, Peru, Japan, and elsewhere; and across Canada.

In Vermont, the utility companies signed a contract with Hydro-Québec even though it was evident that there were cheaper alternatives available. Our three-year battle in Vermont managed only to reduce the size of the contract. Since the contract was signed, however, Vermont has had to pay penalty charges of hundreds of millions of dollars

Left to right: David Dinkins, Mayor of New York City; Matthew Coon Come, Grand Chief of the James Bay Crees; Sappa Fleming, Mayor of Kuujjuarapik (Quebec).

because they have not been able to use the amount of electricity set out in the contract. We don't say "we told you so"; we just say, quietly, that sometimes it pays to listen to Cree wisdom.

In New York, the Crees found allies in Assemblymen William Hoyt and Maurice Hinchey. They took the fight against the New York contracts to the New York Legislature. They called for environmental reviews of the project, even though it was built outside New York State, reasoning that if the purpose of the project was to supply electricity to the state, then such reviews were justified. Their support of this matter was key in Governor Mario Cuomo's decision to call for an analysis of the economic benefit of the contract. The review came out against the contract and it was subsequently dropped. It was the loss of this $17.6 billion contract that caused the governments of Quebec and Canada to agree to an environmental review of the Great Whale Project.

The project was stopped because people recognized the need to protect the pristine environment of Northern Quebec. They saw the dams as a short-term and only partial solution to the need for electrical energy. Moreover, people around the world supported the Crees' right to continue to live on the land, as they had always done. We would not have won the cancellation of those projects, however, if it had not been for the presentation of solutions to the problem of energy supply.

The Grand Council of the Crees demonstrated that there were other cheaper energy generation alternatives to megaprojects like Great Whale. Examples given were energy cogeneration, wind energy, and more modest-sized hydroelectric projects. Their employment study illustrated that the alternatives would create approximately twice the employment that could be created by building a project such as Great Whale.

We had been fighting for an environmental review from the beginning. In 1989, we filed an action in the courts to force the governments of Canada and Quebec to co-operate with the Crees to undertake a review of the project. In 1991, Canada's Environment Minister, Lucien Bouchard, called for a federal review of the project. The province and the federal government then went ahead and agreed to split the project into two parts: the transportation infrastructure ($700 million worth of roads, airports, etc.) versus the project proper. Originally, the Government of Canada said that it did not have to conduct an environmental review under the 1975 Agreement because the project was under Quebec's jurisdiction. We disagreed, as we believed that the social and environmental protection regime under the Agreement was triggered when matters under either federal or provincial jurisdiction were impacted. As we saw it, if there was an impact on fish, Indians, navigable waters, water quality, or migratory waterfowl or marine mammals, then the federal government was required to get involved and a joint federal-provincial review was necessary.

The courts agreed with us. They quashed the federal-provincial agreement to split the project and said that the Crees had the right to a federal and provincial review, or a joint review. We demanded an impartial review process, one that first examined the questions surrounding the justification of the project. A joint federal-provincial Review Secretariat was created to coordinate the review of the project.

Once the review was agreed to, some groups let up on their pressure, but we kept our public campaign going. We wanted the project stopped, not just a review. When New York State cancelled its big contract, Hydro-Québec, the Province of Quebec, and the Government of Canada became serious about undertaking the review and about supplying the Crees and Inuit with some funding to undertake the review as a partner.

The review process was a major undertaking. It took one year just to produce the guidelines, or directives, for Hydro-Québec to write its environmental and social impact statement. However, Hydro-Québec had already written a report and it handed in that report—all 5,000 pages of it—only a couple of months after receiving the directives. Independent experts hired by the Review Secretariat studied the report, and the Crees also engaged experts on issues that we wanted reviewed.

For analysis of the economic "justification" of the project, we relied on two American experts and they showed that, on the one hand, there were more economic benefits for Quebec if an investment equivalent to that proposed for the dam was made in energy conservation and improved efficiency. They also showed that the analysis by Hydro-Québec had been done in a way that skewed the results in favour of the project. The cost of the alternatives had been overestimated.

We took our case to the International Water Tribunal, where our case was joined to that of the infamous China Three Gorges Project—because Hydro-Québec and the Government of Canada were defendants in both cases! After a week of hearings, the Tribunal issued a strong ruling in respect of both projects. They said that both projects were violations of the rights of the affected peasant populations and Indigenous peoples, and they should not be built.

Back in Canada—at the environmental and social assessment processes—the review teams for the Government of Canada, the Province of Quebec, the Inuit, and the Crees criticized the Hydro-Québec environmental and social impact statement for its serious problems with and deficiencies in scientific technique, for almost ignoring the social impacts, and for failing to present a coherent and detailed analysis of the ecological impacts.

We were given no chance to rest as, in 1993, Hydro-Québec proposed to build a modified Eastmain 1 Project. We were still fighting against the Great Whale Project but didn't miss a beat. We objected to the Eastmain 1 Project, stating that the project description had been changed since it was described in the 1975 Agreement. We went to court and, unfortunately, lost. The judge ruled that the project was in fact substantially the same as that described in the Agreement and that it was, therefore, exempt from the requirement for an impact review process. The judge, who had been a lawyer for Hydro-Québec in days gone by, went on to state gratuitously that if natural resource development projects were proposed, only a provincial review needed to be done. His statement meant that impacts on, for example, fish, navigable waters, and Aboriginal rights, which are matters of federal jurisdiction, would not trigger a federal review. In other words, it did not matter how many fisheries or Aboriginal economies were being destroyed, the federal government should not undertake a review of the project as hydro and other resource development are under the jurisdiction of the province. This is not what the Crees agreed to in the 1975 Agreement. Since then, the federal government has simply dropped out of northern Quebec and is avoiding the possibility of being mixed up in any future natural resource development fight.

The Department of Justice is ignoring a decision of record on this very point that we won in Great Whale and is relying instead upon the comments of a judge in a case not on this point to avoid its obligations under the Agreement. Instead of following the obligations of the treaty, the Government of Canada now applies the Canadian Environmental Assessment Act in the James Bay territory, an Act that operates without Cree involvement. Moreover, the officials tell us that Canada prefers the Environmental Assessment Act as, unlike the Agreement process, the Act cannot be used to stop projects.

The 1975 Agreement exempted the La Grande Project from the impact review process. The La Grande Project had originally included the construction of the Eastmain dam, but it was not built in phase one of the project. The Agreement stated that future development must be subject to an impact review process and that both the federal and provincial governments must be involved if matters under their jurisdictions (e.g. water, Aboriginal rights, the environment, animals) are affected by development.

With regard to our battle to stop the Great Whale Project, on November 17, 1994, the day before the report calling for the rewriting of the Hydro-Québec impact statement was made public, Quebec's newly elected premier (Jacques Parizeau) announced that the project was being put on ice. He wanted to get the Crees out of his hair so that he could proceed with his international campaign for Quebec independence. The political cartoon in *Le Devoir* the next day showed Matthew Coon Come with his pants down. In other words, he had lost his public platform.

Le Devoir could not have been more wrong. No sooner had Premier Parizeau torn down the platform built for the Crees by former Premier Bourassa, than he built a new one for us when he announced the coming referendum on sovereignty. I will not go into this here, as you will find it addressed later in this book. I will say, however, that the Crees decided—after an all-Cree commission had toured the Cree communities—to hold their own referendum. We were not going to let others decide to take the Crees and Cree lands out of Canada. Our people ultimately decided that they could not walk or be dragged away, without our consent, from the rights and relationship—however unjust in many respects—that we had historically developed with Canada. As Grand Chief Coon Come said at the time: "We had a choice between embarking in Quebec's canoe, or staying on dry land. We decided to stay on the land."

After the Cree Special Referendum was held, we had the daunting job of trying to piece together our relationship with the Province of Quebec. We also began a process of working with the Government of Canada to look into the outstanding business in the 1975 Agreement and other aspects of our relationship with the federal government.

Then Chief of Waskaganish, Billy Diamond, undertook a process to develop a memorandum of understanding with Quebec on its financial participation in certain community projects. Chief Diamond took the lead because, at that time, the provincial government was reluctant to undertake discussions with the Grand Council of the Crees under the leadership of Grand Chief Coon Come—Quebec believed (paternalistically) that the Grand Council's effective fight against the Great Whale Project, and the Cree Special Referendum were the result of the involvement of non-Cree/Anglophone advisers. Chief Diamond kept the process at the community level. After approximately three years, a memorandum of understanding was signed with Quebec, but the commitments in it were not funded by the Province of Quebec. The province wanted the Crees to borrow the money for the agreed to community projects, and to allow Quebec to provide guarantees to pay back the loans on an annual basis over 10 years! The Crees agreed to this proviso, but this process did not work out very well, and it ended up almost bankrupting some of the communities.

To make matters more difficult, we also had to deal with the forestry regime. When the Agreement was signed in 1975, forestry was a small enterprise in our territory. To protect against the possibility that one day it would expand, we insisted that any forestry activities that affected over 65 square kilometres (25 square miles) would be subject to the environmental review process (which takes a year to complete), while accepting that yearly cutting would be approved within multi-year plans. The Government of Quebec has taken the position that all forestry activities are therefore exempt from review, except for the construction of major access roads and camps.

"Today we have so much forestry. Even in the winter, they continue with the forestry, and there are some animals that just hide in the burrows and holes whenever they feel trouble coming."

Albert Mianscum, 72
Hunter/Trapper

Since 1980, forestry activities have expanded enormously. Companies have moved into the territory in part to allow southern forests to regenerate after years of overcutting. We have seen the impact of this on our hunting way of life. Whole areas hundreds of square miles in size have been clear-cut and have been devoid of animals for years.

For many years, we tried to obtain a regulatory regime that would respect the hunting families' traditional land management techniques, that would be guided by the ecological imperatives of the area, and that would provide employment for the Crees in forestry. All of our recommendations were ignored. Finally, in July 1998, we began a Quebec Superior Court action against the Government of Canada, the Province of Quebec, and the forestry companies in the territory to redress this violation of our treaty rights. In 1999, we realized that the provincial government was about to approve 5- and 25-year management plans that still did not take account of Cree rights. We therefore asked for an injunction on these approvals in a side action to the main case. Mr. Justice Jean-Jacques Croteau of the Quebec Superior Court reserved judgment on the injunction and instead ordered the Province of Quebec to make its Forest Act conform to the rights of the Crees under the treaty. He also stated that he had to make this judgment because he saw a flagrant violation of the Crees' constitutional rights. His decision had the effect of addressing some elements under contention in the main action.

This was a major victory for the Crees. However, the defendants in the main case, including Canada, who had not been party to the injunction on the 5- and 25-year management plans, asked the Chief Justice of the Quebec Superior Court to remove Judge Croteau from the case and to suspend his judgment. They claimed that the judge had been biased in his judgment and had compromised their right to a fair hearing. The Chief Justice decided that the judge had not shown bias, but that he should be removed anyway, just to be fair and avoid any impression of future bias.

This was the first time in Canadian history that the Crown had succeeded in having a judge removed. This was especially galling as this judge had been picked for the case by the Chief Justice, after the defendants had submitted a list of about half of the court's judges whom they considered as having a potential conflict of interest in the case. We appealed the removal of Judge Croteau to the Supreme Court of Canada. They denied leave to appeal the decision, without explanation, and charged court costs to the Crees. We are trying to resolve our differences on forestry with the Government of Quebec outside the courts.

On the federal front, in 1995, we set up a negotiation process with the Government of Canada that was initially headed up by me (as the Cree negotiator) and Michel Vennat, a partner with the Montreal-based law firm Stikeman, Elliott (as the representative for Canada). The process was arranged by Grand Chief Coon Come with then Minister of Indian Affairs Ron Irwin, and it involved a Cree–Canada Round Table of ministers and

Excerpts from a News Release by the Department of Indian Affairs and Northern Development

The Cree-Canada Round Table is intended to promote a government-to-government relationship between the James Bay Cree Nation and Canada, within the Canadian Constitution. Through this process, Canada will be working in partnership with the James Bay Crees, and with Quebec where necessary and possible, in the pursuit of shared objectives.

The round table brings together Cree leaders and ministers of the Government of Canada for co-operative dialogue designed to make the new relationship a lasting reality and to reach agreement on what the Crees and Canada consider priorities for negotiation. The focus of the first meeting was on sustainable economic and social development; healthy, secure, and viable communities; and environmental and social protection.

Cree chiefs. This was to create a new relationship between the Cree Nation and the Government of Canada, and to set the agenda to implement neglected provisions of the 1975 Agreement.

By the time the round table met, a federal election had passed and the new Minister of Indian Affairs and Northern Development, Jane Stewart, brought together a table of ministers with direct obligations under the 1975 Agreement. Not all concerned were present, but the Minister of the Environment (Christine Stewart), the Minister of Human Resources Development (Pierre Pettigrew), and the Solicitor General (Andy Scott) came to the table. Minister Stewart began the discussions with a statement of principle: "The federal government believes that the James Bay Agreement is an important and permanent part of the relationship between the Crees and Canada. The Agreement is to be implemented and the rights preserved, not ticked off or extinguished."

This was a major, historic statement for us. Over the years, the Department of Indian and Northern Affairs had developed the perhaps unwritten policy of demanding that Aboriginal peoples extinguish their treaty rights when they negotiated what was somewhat ironically referred to as an "Implementation Agreement." In the case of the Northern Flood Agreement in Manitoba, the bands that did sign implementation agreements were even required to indemnify the Government of Canada, the Province of Manitoba, and Manitoba Hydro from any claims by anyone stemming from the original Agreement.

In spite of the direction that the round table took, the federal government has since continued to demand that the Crees extinguish their ongoing rights to certain benefits, in exchange for one-time implementation. This was true in the case of police services, fire protection, the Cree Trappers Association, and other issues. In order to obtain long overdue implementation of the 1975 Agreement provisions, we were asked to sign papers that extinguished our rights in the Agreement—we refused. We are continuing the discussions with Canadian and Quebec governments now that I am Grand Chief. It is not clear whether we will be able to achieve the goals that we have set in respect to the Agreement.

We are seeking communities that have adequate housing for all who live there. Today, we still lack 1,500 units and this number is growing at the rate of 100 per year. We are seeking equitable levels of employment in the territory. Today, in 2000, we have less than one percent of the jobs created by development while we make up 45 percent of the territorial population. We also want an environmental and social protection regime, as promised in the Agreement.

As long as our people, and our Indigenous neighbours and friends from coast to coast to coast, remain the most dispossessed, the poorest, the most under-educated and under-housed people with, tragically, the very highest rates of diabetes, tuberculosis, suicide, and despair in this rich land called Canada, then there is still much for us to do.

Accordingly, in December 1998 and March 1999 Cree delegations approached the United Nations Human Rights Committee and the United Nations Committee on Economic, Social and Cultural Rights, and we obtained judgments concerning our international human rights. For the first time, these two bodies—the highest international human rights entities in the international apparatus of the United Nations—formally affirmed that Indigenous peoples in Canada enjoy the rights of peoples contained in the International Human Rights Covenants and the International Bill of Rights. They admonished Canada in the strongest possible terms for its failure to respect these rights, which (they stated) threatened to take Indigenous peoples in Canada to "the brink of political, economic and cultural extinction."

Yet our people are not wallowing in misery, even though conditions are difficult for them. Our people are optimistic, are making progress (in spite of, rather than because of, government help), and are looking forward to the future. This is what it is to be Eeyouch in Eeyou Istchee.

The signing of a treaty is not the end of the story, it is the beginning. What happens to the land, to a way of life, to the language and culture, and ultimately the fate of the Cree people are at stake. We do not know what the future will bring. Our success in whatever we try will depend, in large part, on our ability to seek what is right and what makes sense for the future of our people. Success depends on working together and helping one another. That is who we are, as our name in Cree states: Notchimeeweeyouch, Winnigegoweeyouch Enatimadouch—Inlanders and Coasters Working for Their Mutual Benefit.

Meegwetch!
Grand Chief, Dr. Ted Moses
December 2000

Quebec Secession and Cree Rights: A Background

According to the European concept of colonization, being the first to plant a flag in the name of king/queen and country constituted the right to lay claim to a newly discovered territory, often irrespective of the peoples who already resided there. Thus it was in the 1500s, when both Britain and France planted flags, laid claim, and started fighting over ownership of this place now called Canada. Both European countries sent settlers to colonize the rugged landscape and establish their positions in the "New World."

In 1763, after warring over North American territorial boundaries for 200 years, the British gained possession (through the Treaty of Paris) of the territory known as New France, which they renamed as the Province of Quebec. As early as 1830, the French community in the new province was discussing secession from British rule. In 1867, colonists created the independent country of Canada, a country in which the French in Quebec were guaranteed the right to maintain their French culture including their religion, language, distinct education systems, and a civil law code. Ironically, the Aboriginal cultures that had inhabited the same lands for thousands of years prior to European settlement were not considered or accorded such rights at the time this "new country" was created.

Quebec has had a primarily agricultural history, but in the 20th century the province's economy became more commercial and industrial. At the same time, Quebecers were becoming more urbanized and politicized. During the 1960s, Quebec underwent a period of rapid social, economic, and political change referred to as the "Quiet Revolution." A key element of this modernization process included the provincial government taking a more active role in the provincial economy. In particular, the provincial hydroelectric system (under Hydro-Québec) and access to better education and health services were high priorities on the political agenda, as means for advancing the development of Quebec. Along with these (and other) political and cultural changes came a rise in Quebec nationalism, a nationalism that promoted Quebec's independence from Canada.

In 1975, the Quebec provincial and the federal governments signed the James Bay and Northern Quebec Agreement with the Crees of James Bay. The Quebec Liberal Party of the time saw the Agreement as a way of clearing obstacles to the development and organization of the north. Then in 1976, the Parti Québécois—a party with strong separatist views—was elected in Quebec. In 1978, the fact that the previous provincial government had accepted a federal regime for Cree lands and federal involvement in community and economic development prompted the new provincial government to withdraw from commitments to develop Cree communities. Against this backdrop, the Parti Québécois launched a vigorous campaign to convince Quebecers of the need to

separate from the rest of Canada and to make Quebec an independent nation. A provincial referendum was held on this issue in 1980, and the separatists were defeated—about 60 percent of voters rejected the idea of Quebec independence.

When the 1980 referendum on Quebec sovereignty was held, the Crees and the Inuit of northern Quebec were involved in legal and political initiatives to bring basic housing, sewer, and water services to their communities, as well as to make them players in the regional economy. The treaty promises made to the Crees in 1975—for health services, education services, and economic participation—involved the same rights that Quebecers were demanding for themselves. By not implementing the promises made in the treaty, both Quebec and Canada were seen by the Crees to be in violation of the treaty. After the 1982 repatriation of the Canadian Constitution, the governments' inaction was also seen as a violation of the Crees' constitutional rights. Throughout the 1980s and 1990s, the Crees continued to organize, negotiate, and demand that the provincial and federal governments meet the commitments made in the 1975 Agreement.

In 1995, Quebec separatism was once again brought to the fore by the Parti Québécois. With Quebec again claiming status as a nation, the province threatened to take the Crees and their lands out of Canada. The Crees were no longer willing to let others transfer them from one jurisdiction to another without their input, however, and they decided to become actors in these events.

Relying on international law, the Crees claimed it was their right as peoples to dispose of their resources as they deemed fit and to remain as citizens of Canada, if this was in their best interest. In addition, the Crees published *Sovereign Injustice*, an analysis of Quebec's claim to the right to choose secession from Canada based on their distinct French society and culture. Among other things, the analysis questioned how a province with citizens of multi-ethnic origin could claim rights accorded to peoples (historically determined by the sharing of a common language and culture) under international law.

In conjunction with their appeal to have their rights recognized under international law, and under the strong leadership of Matthew Coon Come (then Grand Chief of the Grand Council of the Crees), the James Bay Crees began to plan their own referendum. This referendum—held just prior to the provincial referendum of October 30, 1995—asked the Eeyouch of Eeyou Istchee to consider whether they would stay with Canada or, pending a separatist win, go with Quebec. The results were dramatic, as the following text will show.

While the Quebec separatists lost the second provincial referendum by less than 1 percent—50.56 percent of Quebecers voted to remain with Canada—polls at the time suggested that more than 15 percent of those who voted for independence would choose to remain in Canada if independence meant carving up the province to recognize Aboriginal rights. Clearly, the strength of the Aboriginal rights issue had been underestimated by Quebec's separatist government. What slips by many observers is that the

Crees' claim of protection under international law, a claim that gave so much credibility to their intervention and that may have saved Canada from splitting up, is vehemently opposed by Canada at the United Nations.

Today, the Parti Québécois remains in power. The province seems once again poised to ask its citizens to consider separating from Canada.

Quebec Secession and Cree Rights

The place was a plush salon of a hotel in downtown Montreal. The date was October 25, 1995, the day after the first Cree referendum on Quebec secession.

For a media conference, the 9:00 a.m. hour was quite early, but the room was packed solid with dozens of journalists and television cameras from Quebec, elsewhere in Canada, and internationally. The event was being carried live on Newsworld and its French language equivalent on Radio Canada.

A tired and somewhat crumpled Grand Chief Matthew Coon Come entered the room at 9:05 a.m., with Quebec spokesman Romeo Saganash. They had just flown south from the James Bay seat of Cree government in Nemaska, immediately after the ballot count for the Cree referendum had been completed at 4:00 a.m.

Grand Chief Coon Come announced the results of this historic plebiscite among his people. His remarks are worthy of reproduction in full.

Wachiya!

I am Grand Chief Matthew Coon Come. I have just learned the results, and now so will you. My people, Eeyouch, the James Bay Crees, voted yesterday not to be separated from Canada.

We have spoken. We have spoken clearly. We have spoken in our own voice. We have spoken on our own territory. We have spoken as our own people. We have spoken as unanimously as a people possibly can.

The message is clear, and now others must listen.

We will not be separated from Canada. We have withheld our consent. The message is clear: We Won't Go.

Let me state at the outset, as I have done before: we Crees understand the aspirations of Quebecers. We fully respect their right to hold consultative referendums and determine their future.

But I must also state that this cannot, and will not, be done at the expense of our rights, or of the rights of other peoples in Canada. We Crees have the selfsame right to our aspirations and to determine our future. Quebec would never agree to be forcibly included in the results of a majority vote in Canada. We Crees cannot agree to be forcibly included in the results of a single majority referendum in Quebec. The message is clear; my people have made their choice: We and our territory will not be forcibly included in an independent Quebec.

Let me explain this choice to you, and how this choice was made.

In October, it is already winter in James Bay. It is already snowing in James Bay, and the hunting season is underway. In James Bay, from September to spring, we Crees are out hunting on the land. Our communities are often ghost towns at this time of year.

This year, on October 24, things were different. From hundreds of kilometres away, people made their way back to our communities. Yesterday, in Mistissini, in Chisasibi, in Whapmagoostui, and in Wemindji, they made their way to our polling stations in our schools and our meeting halls.

There were lineups, and some people waited an hour or two to vote. There were voting stations in every community. There were voting stations outside our territory, in Montreal, in Val d'Or, in Senneterre, in Ottawa, and even in North Bay in Ontario, where our post-secondary students are studying.

There were Cree families in their hunting camps that were too far away in the bush to get back to the communities. Our territory is not covered by a network of roads and telephone services. These families were contacted by radio. They were asked to provide their co-ordinates and to stay in their camps between Friday, October 20 and Tuesday, October 24. In order to ensure that every Cree had a chance to vote, we chartered three helicopters, which flew thousands of kilometres across our territory, until last night.

Imagine if [Premier] Parizeau had called a referendum at the end of July, when Quebecers are on the beaches and touring in Quebec and elsewhere. We were forced to do the equivalent: our referendum could not have been held at a more difficult time. And yet, under these conditions, over 77 percent of eligible Crees participated in our vote. And more importantly, they have made their choice abundantly clear.

The Cree NO majority was not a 50 percent plus 1 vote, such as [Premier] Parizeau and Mr. Bouchard [leader of the federal Bloc Québécois] say is enough to break up a country. We have spoken more clearly than that.

The Cree NO majority was not a 60 percent vote. We have spoken more clearly than that.

The Cree NO majority was not a 70 percent vote. We have spoken more clearly than that.

The Cree NO majority was not a 80 percent vote. We have spoken more clearly than that.

The Cree people were almost unanimous: over 96 percent of my people have stated their choice. We Won't Go.

What does this mean? The separatists will say that our Cree referendum is all very well, but it does not count. We Crees and our lands, they say, are to be forcibly included in the majority vote. And then, they state calmly, we Crees and our territory are to be forcibly included, if necessary by force, in a sovereign Quebec.

Well, let me say calmly in reply: the Crees have spoken—We Won't Go.

To forcibly separate us from Canada would be unconstitutional.

To forcibly separate us from Canada would be illegal.

To forcibly separate us from Canada would be undemocratic.

To forcibly take us out of one country and into another would be a breach of our human rights. This would be the kidnapping of the James Bay Crees. This would be the hijacking of a whole people and their lands. This we will not allow the separatists to do.

The James Bay Crees have spoken clearly: We Will Not Go.

A few days ago, the Parti Québécois chief spokesman on Aboriginal issues said that the Crees will be violating the law, violating international law, if we resist our inclusion in his independent Quebec.

I find this truly ironic. Here we have a separatist government of a province contemplating an illegal and unconstitutional secession. The Superior Court of Quebec has already ruled that the [Parti Québécois's] Bill 1 is illegal and unconstitutional. The Superior Court of Quebec has already ruled that the [party's] plans are a grave threat to the rights and freedoms of Quebec citizens.

No, Mr. Parizeau. No, Mr. Bouchard.

The James Bay Crees have spoken. We will resist the violation of our treaty rights. We will resist the violation of our constitutional rights. We will resist the violation of our human rights. And in doing so, my people will be upholding the law. We will be upholding Canadian law. We will be upholding international law. We will be upholding the universal principles of equality of peoples, and respect for their rights. We will be upholding the democratic wishes of a people who have lived here, and governed themselves on this land, for thousands of years. We will be upholding the Constitution and the rule of law.

We will be challenging the law of the jungle. We will be challenging the tyranny of the self-declared rights of a majority over the fundamental rights of others. We will be challenging the discrimination, the double standards, the manipulation, and the use of force.

There is no international law right to hold a revolution. And yet what the separatists are proposing is just that. There is no international law right of insurrection. And yet, what the separatists are proposing is just that. There is no international law right to break up existing states. In fact, international law forbids these things.

Both the Meech Lake Accord (1990) and the Charlottetown Accord (1992) were failed attempts by the federal government to reform the Canadian Constitution. The reforms would have, among other things, accommodated Quebec as a distinct society. Among the provisions of the Charlottetown Accord there was also a recognition of Aboriginal peoples' inherent right of self-government within Canada. Neither accord was ratified.

And yet, it is the separatists who are proposing a unilateral declaration of independence, an insurrection, the breakup of an existing state—all in violation of international law.

The best they can say is, we will exercise effective control, by force if necessary, and then we will be independent. And the separatists are accusing the Indians of threatening to break international law! Once again, one standard for Quebecers, another for Indigenous peoples.

My people have spoken. We are no longer prepared to be treated like cattle in a field. We are no longer prepared to be treated like a second-class people, with second-class rights. We showed at Meech, and we showed at Charlottetown, that the politics of exclusion and the politics of denial are no longer acceptable.

My people have spoken. They have expressed their will. We will no longer allow decisions to be made by others that are ours, and only ours, to make.

In the last few weeks, I have received many calls from Aboriginal leaders across the country. They are watching this situation with alarm. We Crees have a treaty with Canada. Our treaty rights are entrenched in Section 35 of the Constitution. The Aboriginal leaders in the rest of Canada are saying, "If the Crees' treaty rights, if the Crees' constitutional rights, can be disposed of just like that, then so can ours!"

Please hear me: there will be outrage across the rest of Canada, from the East Coast to the West, from the American border to the Arctic, if Aboriginal peoples see the James Bay Crees and other First Peoples in Quebec being hijacked and forcibly included into a sovereign Quebec.

My people have voted. We are saying: We Won't Go. We Won't Go. We Won't Go.

This is not Matthew Coon Come alone speaking out. This is all of the Crees. This is not the Crees alone. Listen carefully, and you will hear the other First Nations and First Peoples of Quebec. There is a fundamental problem here. We know our rights. We intend to defend our rights. We Won't Go. And neither will our lands, and neither will the hydroelectric and other natural resources they contain.

I am always asked, so I may as well answer the question in advance: Will the Crees become violent? We are not a violent people. We oppose the use of force and have always found other means of resolving our differences. The use of violence and force is against our fundamental beliefs.

We Crees are committed to working together with Quebecers and other Canadians, to building a country that is responsive to all our aspirations and priorities, and that is fully respectful of all our rights.

But we will not be passive in any strategies of inequality and unilateral action. We know our rights. We know we will receive the support of many Quebecers, and the support of other Canadians. We will not be forcibly included in a sovereign Quebec. Our traditional territory, Eeyou Istchee, will not be forcibly removed from Canada and included in a sovereign Quebec. Our human rights will be upheld.

Ron Irwin, federal Minister of Indian Affairs [and Northern Development] said yesterday that the land [ceded to Quebec in] 1898, that is our land, is different. He affirmed that the Aboriginal peoples' voice is a significant part of the situation.

We will use the courts. We will gather the support of Canadians. We will approach the international community.

And in the end, We Won't Go.

The room was silent for a surprisingly long moment, and then the sense of shock was broken by a well-known journalist for the Quebec daily newspaper *La Presse:* "Monsieur Coon Come," she called out, "is this your declaration of war?"

The reply was vintage Matthew. "Madam," said Coon Come, flashing his trademark grin, "these were ballots, not bullets. If you can't tell the difference between an exercise of democratic will and an act of war only because it is exercised by Indians, then your society has a major problem."

Just months earlier, Quebec Premier Jacques Parizeau had announced the shelving of the Great Whale hydroelectric megaproject after a ferocious five-year international campaign against it by Grand Chief Coon Come and the Cree people. *La Presse* had published an editorial cartoon showing a confused Coon Come, feather in hair and tomahawk held aloft, but with his pants around his ankles and a pair of polka-dotted briefs dominating the landscape. The implication: this would mark the defeat and end of Cree campaigner Coon Come.

Little did *La Presse* know; Coon Come and the Eeyouch did not miss a beat. With the deck cleared of Great Whale—no doubt a move that was part of Mr. Parizeau's political calculus in the lead-up to his 1995 secession referendum (he thought he could thus rid himself of the internationally pesky Coon Come)—the Crees were able to focus their attention wholly on the other key issue they had been working on for some years, namely their rights in the context of the possible secession of Quebec from Canada.

Cree work on this issue had begun belatedly, at the Cree Nation General Assembly in the community of Mistissini in 1989. There had been a separatist government in power in Quebec from 1976 to 1985, but proactive Cree political capacity had been limited because the Crees were fully engaged in the development challenges facing their people in the shadow of the La Grande hydro project. This project had devastated their lands, waters, and traditional economies and, despite their signing of the James Bay and Northern Quebec Agreement of 1975, implementation of the agreement conditions were not progressing well.

By 1989, however, separatist rumblings were re-emerging. Grand Chief Coon Come was directed to formulate a detailed Cree position on the Crees' rights in this context and to take all necessary steps to assert and defend their rights. By 1992, detailed research had been undertaken by Cree leaders and lawyers, and an initial draft of a legal study—*Sovereign Injustice*—was tabled by the Grand Council of the Crees at the United Nations in Geneva.

The Royal Commission on Aboriginal Peoples was established in 1991 by the federal government. The most expensive royal commission to date, it reported in 1996. The five-volume report called for a "fundamental reorganization of the country's social and political institutions in relation to Aboriginal peoples." In the commissioners' words: "We advocate recognition of Aboriginal nations within Canada as political entities through which Aboriginal people can express their distinctive identity within the context of Canadian citizenship....At the heart of our recommendations is the recognition that Aboriginal peoples are peoples, that they form collectives of unique character, and that they have a right to governmental autonomy."

This detailed brief laid out a case of separatist double standards, of asserting a right of self-determination under international law for a "Peuple Québécois" while denying that selfsame right to the Cree people; of Government of Quebec threats to use force against Aboriginal peoples to forcibly include them in an independent Quebec; and of the Crees' strong case that under Canadian constitutional law and international law, the Cree people have the right to determine their own political future in a context of any separation of the Province of Quebec from Canada.

Predictably, the Crees' United Nations brief had been met with outrage by the Government of Quebec. As for the federal government, signals were received that this effort was not appreciated and the Crees were quietly warned that they risked fanning the flames of separatism and that they should desist. The English press seemed to agree with the federal Crown. While generally silent, Québécois academics were less dismissive; a number seemed to acknowledge with some embarrassment that the Crees had a point—if Quebecers were a people with a right to separate, the Crees were more so and had the right to choose to remain with Canada, with their lands and the dams that were on them.

This was also the era of extensive hearings by the Royal Commission on Aboriginal Peoples. The Crees were invited to address a special hearing of the Commission in Montreal, chaired by Mr. Justice René Dussault of the Quebec Court of Appeal. Justice Dussault had indicated that he wished the Crees to speak about self-government; the Crees indicated in response that this was to be an Aboriginal-driven commission and that they intended to raise their concerns about Quebec secession. Tabling *Sovereign Injustice* with Justice Dussault, they called for the Commission to undertake studies into these questions, which it ultimately did, reluctantly it seemed. In spite of the profound human rights implications of the issue, the Commission's final report never made mention of these studies.

The Grand Council of the Crees took a leading role in another key area of Aboriginal politics: the community of First Nations in Quebec. The Assembly of First Nations of Quebec and Labrador can be thought of as an Aboriginal version of the United Nations, on a much smaller scale, of course. It is the collective representative of the 10 First Nations in Quebec. Addressing political issues that have an impact on the collective well-being of Aboriginal peoples in Quebec, the Assembly is made up of the chiefs from each community within the 10 First Nations in the province. A historic declaration was issued unanimously by these nations at Lac Delage in October 1994. Its dramatic import is self-explanatory.

Declaration of the First Nations of Quebec and Labrador

The Nations of this region do solemnly declare that our rights and freedoms flow from our ancestral homelands;

Let it be further declared that portions of our lands have been treatied by our forefathers giving access but not ownership or exclusive sovereignty over our territories;

We affirm the Nation-to-Nation relationship based on equality and peaceful co-existence of peoples;

We reject and dismiss the concept of territorial integrity of Quebec;

We will consider our options;

Only we, the Indigenous Peoples, will determine the future of our children on the principle of equality and peaceful co-existence;

We are not attacking Quebecers and we do not intend to;

We will defend our right to choose whom we want to be associated with;

Relations with non-Aboriginal governments will reflect our inherent rights as Peoples and Nations;

Any change to the political constitutional framework requires Aboriginal consent;

Our First Nations will resist any attempt by any government to deny our rights or to deprive those rights of the recognition and protection enjoyed by the First Nations Peoples.

Thus it was with the campaign for Quebec secession underway and Premier Parizeau announcing his October 30, 1995 referendum. Everybody, except other First Nations and the Cree people themselves, seemed to be telling the Cree leadership to shut up and leave the important business of dealing with secession to the governments of Quebec and Canada.

In the summer of 1994, the Cree Nations had mandated Grand Chief Coon Come to hold the Crees' own referendum on Quebec secession, in the event that it became necessary by clear deed to demonstrate the Crees' refusal to be included in a Quebec majority on this issue. The importance of this Cree referendum mandate was soon clearly confirmed by the tabling, in the National Assembly, of the separatist government's Bill 1. This proposed law affirmed a God-given right of Quebecers to "their" territory—intact all the way up to the northern shores of Ungava Bay and Hudson Bay—and also once again declared the existence of a single "Peuple Québécois" (that somehow included subject Aboriginal nations whose interests it promised to protect, but who were forced along for the ride, whether they liked it or not!).

As the 1995 pre-secession referendum debate heated up in Quebec, the Crees relentlessly exposed the discriminatory double standard inherent in this argument, through intensive participation in National Assembly hearings, newspaper articles, and speeches in Canada and internationally.

Importantly, the Grand Council of the Crees refused to participate in the Government of Quebec's secession commission's "road show" hearings, which were designed to drum up support for the separatist cause. It did so because it had put in place the Crees' own Eeyou Istchee Commission, which held hearings in all of the Cree communities and in Montreal, Quebec City, and a number of other centres.

The Eeyou Istchee Commission disclosed a high level of Cree consensus on and commitment to the position that had been articulated by the Grand Council to date: the Cree people were absolutely certain that they had always had, and still had, the right of self-determination. Further, they were determined to affirm and exercise this right in the present secessionary context.

International legitimacy was the emerging battleground for the Government of Quebec, which was claiming that its right to secede was a right inherent in all peoples and, thus, the single Quebec people. Chillingly, it was being asserted that the Crees' northern lands would accrue to an independent Quebec—one that would make a unilateral declaration of independence and assert "effective control," by force if necessary, over all the North including the Aboriginal peoples therein.

The Grand Council determined that it would have to act more effectively than ever before in the international arena. Accordingly, Grand Chief Matthew Coon Come addressed all forums at which there were opportunities to address key decision-makers, particularly in the United States and France. These two states, the Crees reasoned, would be key in the hours and days that followed a possible YES vote in a Quebec referendum. These venues included speaking dates at the prestigious Center for Strategic and International Studies in Washington, D.C., the Harvard Center for International Affairs, and the Kennedy School of Government.

At the same time, the Crees' *Sovereign Injustice* brief had been augmented to become a major legal and political analysis of over 500 pages. In the weeks before the October 1995 provincial referendum, the Grand Council moved rapidly to publish and dispatch over 2,500 copies, by courier, to law and politics libraries, state departments, academics, and courts around the world. The foreword to the book, which is reproduced here, was acclaimed by a number of international scholars but never responded to by separatist militants. It encapsulated the entire dramatic situation.

Foreword to *Sovereign Injustice*

We are Eeyouch. We are a people. We have our own land, Eeyou Istchee. We are an organized society of Aboriginal people forming part of the community of the world's Indigenous peoples. We are the original inhabitants of our territory, and have occupied our land and governed ourselves for the past 9,000 years.

At least four times—in 1670, 1870, 1898, and 1912—Eeyou Istchee, our traditional lands and waters, have changed status, purportedly, transferred between kings as gifts or deeded between colonial companies and governments, all without our knowledge and certainly without our consent. It has always been assumed that we, the James Bay Crees, the actual owners and occupants, simply passed with the land, without voice, without the right to determine or even know what was being done with us.

Now in 1995, although we live in a modern and democratic state, protected by the Canadian Constitution with its Charter of Rights and Freedoms, our people and our territory may once again be transferred from sovereign to sovereign, this time from Canada to what may become the newly independent state of Quebec. And although there is now a United Nations, with a Universal Declaration of Human Rights and a vast array of international human rights instruments that should protect us, a process has been set in motion that would forcibly remove the Crees from Canada, and incorporate us and our lands in this new state.

What is our remedy against this threat to deprive us of our rights, status, and interests—to hand a whole people over against its democratic will to another state? What action can we, the Crees, take now to prevent this assault on democracy and human rights?

This book holds part of the answer. Herein we set out our rights as the Cree people, as one of the world's Indigenous peoples, as citizens of Canada and residents of Quebec, as a people with internationally protected human rights. This is a timely call to avoid the tragic repetition of history, to invoke fairly and democratically the principles of equality and non-discrimination and to respect the Crees' right to self-determination.

Although this book has it origins in the possible separation of Quebec from Canada, its scope extends far beyond the Quebec referendum into the future of the Crees in Canada as a self-governing people. It explores our rights as a people bound to Canada by a treaty and the land itself, and it examines our right of self-determination as it pertains to our aspirations and our rights to share equally in the development of our country.

The myth persists in Quebec and elsewhere in Canada, that this country consists of two founding nations of peoples. This fiction constitutes a practical denial of our presence, our rights and status and our role in the history, economy, and well-being of this country.

Now, as Canada debates its own possible disintegration, many would prefer once again to conduct this debate without facing the troubling and far-reaching questions regarding our rights as an Aboriginal people. Many Aboriginal peoples would also prefer to stay in the background and allow the "non-Natives" to fight this out among themselves.

For the Crees, this is no longer possible. It is our people and our own land that are being threatened, and the Crees must be heard or we may become the victims of our own silence, passed along with the land.

It will become clear when you read this book that we have been making extensive preparations to defend ourselves. We know our rights, and we can reply strongly to every one of the many false arguments that have been made by those who consider it in their own interest to deny our rights. This debate will continue in Canada—the

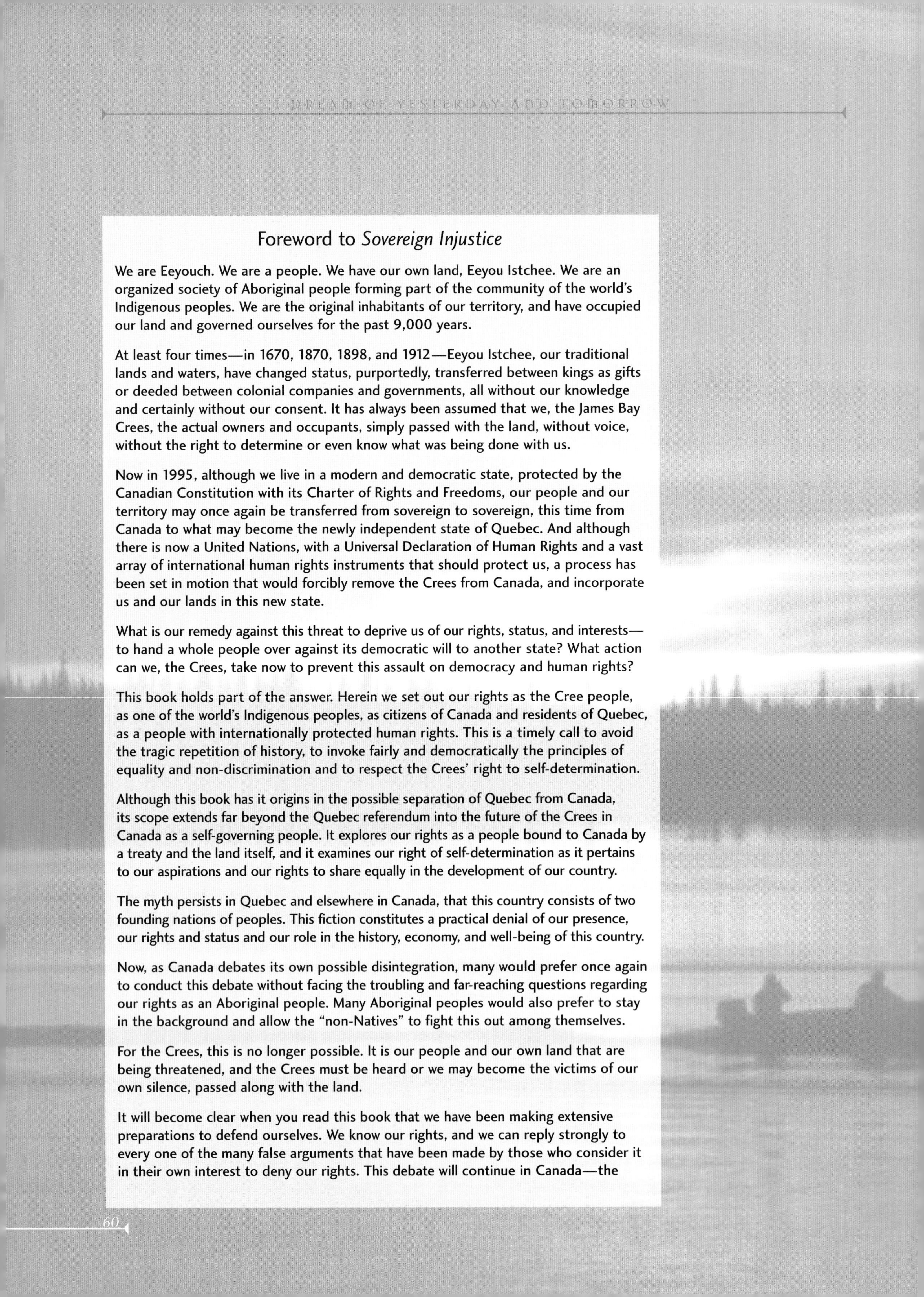

need to recognize and respect the rights of the Crees and other Aboriginal peoples in order to advance the well-being of all of its citizens, to strengthen its democracy, its respect for human rights, and its future as a country that includes Aboriginal peoples in its own vision of itself.

That has not yet happened. Perhaps the unity debate, and the examination of Cree rights and status that it brings into focus, will help to bring this about. That is certainly one of our goals, and perhaps the most important reason to read this study.

In any case, this is certain: the Crees will be here. We are not going anywhere. Nothing will be done with us, now or in the future, without our informed consent.

In the months and weeks before the Crees' own referendum, the Grand Council of the Crees made strenuous efforts to persuade the senior federal government officials advising Jean Chrétien that it was in Canada's interest to declare that yes, the Crees were a party to a three-way, constitutionally guaranteed and affirmed federal arrangement embodied in the 1975 James Bay and Northern Quebec Agreement (signed by the governments of Canada and Quebec, and by the Crees and the Inuit). The Grand Council also worked to convince them that, if Quebecers voted to secede, the Crees had the right to insist that the Crown uphold their treaty relationship with Canada.

The reason for these efforts was simple: the Grand Council of the Crees had recently commissioned a nationwide poll, using the federal Liberal Party's own pollsters, concerning Canadians' and Quebecers' attitudes to the arguments being raised by the Crees. The results were remarkable, for two key reasons.

The referendum question posed to Quebecers was: "Do you agree that Quebec should become sovereign, after having made a formal offer to Canada for a new economic and political partnership, within the scope of the Bill respecting the future of Quebec and of the agreement signed on 12 June 1995?"

The Bill referred to is Bill 1, which described the future of Quebec and declared its sovereignty, and the agreement of 12 June 1995 was the agreement between the two provincial separatist parties, the Parti Québécois and the Action démocratique du Québec.

First, it became clear that the federal government's polls were asking the wrong question about Quebecers' opinions regarding secession: they were polling about full independence. This option was indeed a loser and appears, in retrospect, to be one reason that Prime Minister Chrétien was so nonchalant about the possibility of losing a referendum vote until just days before the referendum. However, this was not the question before Quebecers. The results, when respondents were asked a soft question full of terms of association with Canada—exactly the question Premier Parizeau finally asked—were too chillingly close to call.

Second, the Cree poll asked Quebecers about their voting intentions and whether they would change them if the federal government declared that it would uphold the rights of the Crees to choose to remain with Canada. In short, would separatists continue to support secession if it appeared that an independent Quebec would be a much smaller place, namely a Quebec without the northern two-thirds, which were transferred to it in 1898 and 1912 and which are Cree and Inuit traditional lands. The results of the poll were dramatic: of the half of the Quebecers polled who said that they supported secession, almost one-third (15 percent) indicated that they would change their vote to NO if it was affirmed by the courts, the United Nations, or the Crown that the Crees indeed had the right to choose to remain in Canada—with their lands—if Quebecers voted to secede.

The poll results were also dramatic in indicating Quebecers' and other Canadians' support for the Crees' position. In Quebec, all federalists and 60 percent of separatists accepted the Crees' argument that if Quebecers had a right to separate, the Crees had the right to decide to stay. Outside Quebec, between 90 percent (in Ontario) and 98 percent (in British Columbia) of Canadians declared their support for the Crees. Not surprisingly, hundreds of letters and calls of support from ordinary Canadians began to pour into the Grand Council of the Crees' Ottawa office.

It was now as clear as daylight to the Crees that they were the linchpin holding the country together. It became equally clear, and remains very clear, that those in control of the official approach of the federal government would rather lose a good country than ever have to rely on Indians to help save it.

Cutting Into the Cree System of Land Management

For more than a thousand years, the Crees of the James Bay territory have had a unique system of land and resource management. Through this long history of subsistence living, the Crees have developed a philosophy rooted in respect for the bounty of the land, and an understanding that survival depends on careful harvesting of hunting territories. Only in this way, they believe, will the fish, game, and wood remain plentiful for their next return. Traditional hunting lands are passed on through lines of family and kinship, but are also shared with other families. A hunting group's ouchimaw keeps track of harvesting activities to ensure that the family territory has enough fish and game to support the group. In modern terms, the ouchimaw is the equivalent of a resource manager or game warden, determining where and when hunting can occur and who can harvest how much.

Look at the trees and rivers out there. That is my school. All the animals, all the fish in the river, was my classroom.

William Ratt, "I am very old"
Hunter/Trapper

The Cree ethic of sustainable resource management extends to the everyday activities of any Cree group going into the bush. Like many other Aboriginal peoples, the Crees do not waste any part of an animal that has been killed for food. All is eaten, even a moose's nostrils!

It is the belief that you have to respect the animals. All the bones used to be hung on a platform so that the animals couldn't get at them. And nothing was ever wasted. We used to boil the bones and drink the liquid. It gives you energy. Just about everything in the animal was eaten. One of the ways that we used to store the food to make it last longer was to dry the meat and make jerky out of it.

John Mianscum, "more than 65"
Hunter/Trapper

The floors of Cree tents are typically lined with spruce boughs, which make a soft floor and fill the tent with a pleasant odour. A few boughs, carefully chosen and no more than a few feet in length, are snipped from many trees. Too much taken from one tree would damage it. This practice shows respect for the tree and for others who may camp in the same place later, and will also need to harvest nearby trees to make a covering for their tent floors. Trees are also cut and stripped to make the tent frame. When a hunting group moves on, they leave the frame behind for the next group or the next time they visit the spot.

Despite the numerous changes the Crees have experienced over the past millennium, including the development of permanent communities, the system of family hunting territories and its associated customs of use remain in place today. This system is still a cornerstone of Cree culture.

According to Cree elders, logging companies began cutting in their traditional territory in the early 1960s. In these years, logging operations were conducted mainly during the winter months and horse teams hauled the wood out to the road or rail for shipping. Although chainsaws had replaced axes and crosscut saws by this time, logging was still labour-intensive and crews of men were needed to cut and limb the trees, and to load the logs onto sleighs and then onto trucks and trains. At the time, the Crees served as a readily available labour source, and many Cree men camped with their families near the operations during logging season. Then, using the money from logging, they would buy provisions and head out to their hunting territories for the remainder of the year.

The Crees maintained this mutually beneficial relationship with logging until the early 1970s. As tractors and skidders replaced the horse teams and feller-bunchers supplanted chainsaws, the nature of work in the logging industry changed. Cree men were no longer needed in the face of this mechanization of the industry and, for the most part, the benefits that the Crees had derived from forestry ended. By 1999, fewer than one percent of Crees were employed in the logging industry.

With modern logging machinery able to churn out more and more wood at the roadside, the capacity of pulp mills and sawmills in the region increased. An exponential increase in the construction of intrusive road networks allowed year-round logging operations to occur. By the late 1970s and early 1980s, Cree family hunting territories in the southern part of Eeyou Istchee (at the 49th parallel), near the community of Waswanipi, were left barren by extensive clear-cutting and road building.

From the mid-1980s to the present, the logging industry has continued its growth in Eeyou Istchee, and more family hunting territories are being affected by these activities each year. Capital investment in wood production facilities in and adjacent to the James Bay territory grew from 13.1 percent of the provincial total in 1983 to 57.7 percent in 1988. This growth in capital investment coincided with the passage of the Forest Act in 1986, which ushered in a whole new forestry regime in Quebec. It is estimated that the amount of land cleared annually has increased from 400 square kilometres (154 square miles) in 1985 to over 800 square kilometres (309 square miles) in 1999. Currently, more than 90 Cree family hunting territories from five different communities have suffered logging-related disturbances, and cutting has moved further north, toward the 52nd parallel.

Undoubtedly, the most disruptive aspect of forestry exploitation in the boreal forest is the use of extensive clear-cutting. Because the average tree height and diameter of the northern black spruce is much less than that of southern tree species, such as red or white pine, logging companies operating in the boreal forest cannot afford to be selective in their cutting. Add to this the extensive road networks that must be built over difficult terrain to cover the lengthy distances to the processing mills, and the economic benefits of this type of logging are marginal. Companies must clear as much forest as possible in the shortest time possible to make up for their required upfront investment. This is why clear-cutting is the only practical method of logging for the industry in the James Bay territory.

The result of this economic reality is several thousand square kilometres of clear-cut forests. Conservatively, the Crees estimate that a total of more than 15,540 square kilometres (6,000 square miles) has been cleared since the signing of the James Bay and

Waswanipi Cree Model Forest Project

The heart is being cut out of the Waswanipi band's traplines by the clear-cutting of the forest where these hunters and trappers have always derived their livelihood. A model forest project has been set up as a response to the increasing grip that outsiders have gained over Waswanipi's traditional lands.

A group of Aboriginal, government, academic, and industry partners established the project. Its objective has been to ensure that the forest continues to be managed according to traditional Cree management practices.

Northern Quebec Agreement in 1975. Current provincial regulations allow for clear-cutting in large blocks of up to 150 hectares (371 acres). The regulations stipulate, however, that tree buffers of at least 100.6 metres (110 yards) in width must separate adjoining blocks of clear-cut areas. The net effect of these cutting regulations is a landscape of large, nearly continuous clear-cuts (often hundreds of square kilometres in size), separated by football field-sized buffers.

Obviously, clear-cutting thousands of square kilometres of forest in large, nearly continuous blocks results in substantial habitat loss. The remaining buffer strips between clear-cut blocks—and the prescribed 20-metre (22-yard) forested buffers around lakes, rivers, and streams—provide little alternative habitat to sustain the area's natural resources. Beyond these buffers, there is little protection from logging for the fish and game in the northern boreal forest.

Recent changes to Quebec's forestry regulations have further reduced the amount of protected habitat. Prior to 1996, licence holders were required to set aside, in addition to cut-block buffers, a minimum of 4 percent of the area to manage as moose yards. These yards, designed to offer more protection for moose, especially in the winter months, were to be located in stands of trees of various ages and species throughout the cutting areas. Also in the old regulations, beaver habitat was protected by the above-mentioned 20-metre buffers around watercourses, plus an additional 200-metre (219-yard) buffer upstream from any beaver dams. When the forestry regulations were revised in 1996, both of these habitat provisions were removed without replacement. Beaver and moose are the two most important animals to Cree hunters, and yet there are no specific provisions in the forestry regulations to protect them.

We were never told [about] anything that was going to happen on the land, like the clear-cutting. It just happened.

I wish you were in my shoes, and you could appreciate how much it hurts. When you are powerless, [you feel] the frustration of doing nothing when what little traplines we have left are just being pulled away on the back of logging trucks. Those are our traplines on the back of those trucks!

Isaac Dixon, 79
Hunter/Trapper

The rapid escalation of logging occurring in Eeyou Istchee is having dire consequences for the subsistence activities of Cree hunters. Small and large game, birds, and fish that reside in the northern boreal forest ecosystem are primary sources of food for these hunters, but these animals are being displaced by the cumulative effects of thousands of square kilometres of clear-cuts and road networks. In the southern part of Eeyou Istchee, moose are a primary source of food. There has already been a well-documented collapse in the moose population in the areas most heavily logged.

Even before provisions to protect moose habitat were removed from the Quebec forestry regulations, Cree hunters began warning of an impending crash in the moose population in the areas most actively logged. After intense lobbying by the Crees, the provincial government agreed to undertake an aerial moose survey. The results indicated that there had been a steep decline in numbers of moose. In 1985, provincial wildlife managers had estimated the population of moose in the southern part of the James Bay territory to be 1,200. By 1995, estimates were 400. Recent studies indicated that the moose appear to be migrating further north, into areas as yet untouched by logging activities. Cree hunters north of traditional moose habitat regions have corroborated this migration. Despite the recognition by provincial wildlife managers (from the Ministry of Environment) of a serious decline in the moose population, no special arrangements have been made or constraints placed on logging companies to try to reverse this trend.

There's a big difference between what the water tasted like a few years ago and what it tastes like today. Even the meat tastes different. The majority of our food is taken from this water. The moose tastes different because it eats plants from the water. I can taste the difference in water between the bottom and the top of the lake. Today, I know that's a big difference, the taste of the water.

Isaac Dixon, 79
Hunter/Trapper

Another disastrous side effect of clear-cutting has been soil erosion. The heavy machinery used in modern logging practices disrupts the soil and leaves behind deep ruts that, especially in low-lying areas, are often the source of erosion. Much of the soil is washed into roadside ditches and finds its way into nearby watercourses. Cree hunters consistently comment that local fish stocks, muskrats, moose, otters, and beaver are all affected by soil erosion and the associated siltation of small watercourses.

Despite the existence of specific regulations concerning standards for roads, bridges, and culverts, further soil erosion is caused by improper road construction, particularly use of improper bridging materials and undersized drainage culverts. Logging roads cross thousands of creeks, small streams, rivers, and small lakes—drainage and associated erosion problems are found throughout the territory. The vast majority of logging roads are not subjected to any environmental impact assessments or regular government inspections.

The Crees of the eastern James Bay region have long defined themselves as a forest people, or Notchimeeweeyouch in Cree. Fully one-third of the over 12,000 Crees in this region live primarily from what the land provides. Recognizing the high level of unemployment in Cree communities (often above 40 percent), the Crees estimate that another one-third of this population participates in a mixed subsistence/seasonal employment economy. Much like the Crees who worked in forestry during the times of the crosscut saw and chainsaws, this segment of the Cree population relies on fish and game to help make ends meet during periods when no other employment is available.

Every year, Cree families are displaced from their traditional hunting territories because of rapidly expanding forestry activities. When this is explained to government and forestry company officials, they respond by telling the Crees not to worry, those areas will have many new trees growing within 10 to 20 years. The Crees question the effectiveness of the forest managers' reliance on natural regeneration techniques, which makes this claim highly suspect. Further, these officials fail to recognize that 10 to 20 years represents nearly a generation of young Crees who will not benefit from the hundreds of years of traditional subsistence knowledge that has been passed down through the generations. This knowledge is the fabric of Cree culture and, without the forest classroom in which to share and foster this knowledge, the culture is lost.

I know that White people have great philosophies on [the] environment. They write extensively on bylaws, rules, and acts. But you don't see it in application.

So when I sit with my children and my family, we talk about what's happened. My son will say to me: "Did you know that such-and-such a river, you can't go up anymore?" If there's a spawning area in that river, they would say they were going to do their best to minimize the impact on that spawning area, but in fact they pay no attention.

So there is mistrust now that is much higher than it ever was—when you see the forest sitting in front of you saying things.

Johnny Cooper
Project Manager,
Waswanipi Model Forest Project

The Peace of the Brave: A Landmark Agreement

Without adequate lands and resources, Aboriginal nations will be unable to build their communities and structure the employment opportunities necessary to achieve self-sufficiency.... Currently on the margins of Canadian society, they will be pushed to the edge of economic, cultural, and political extinction.

Report of the Royal Commission on Aboriginal Peoples, 1996

On February 7, 2002, the James Bay Crees achieved another first in advancing the rights of Aboriginal peoples. They signed a landmark agreement with the Province of Quebec, taking them a critical step closer to true self-sufficiency. With the Peace of the Brave—the New Agreement—the Crees have advanced further in the achievement of their goal of self-determination. They have achieved the means to benefit from development of their communities and traditional lands.

As with everything Cree, the story is an interesting one. It is a complex tale of long-standing conflicts, confidential negotiations, fervent disagreements, and visionary solutions. It is the tale of a spirited people who have raised the standard for Aboriginal-government negotiations in Canada, have broken new ground with their fight for self-determination, and are finally standing on common ground with their enduring opponent, the Government of Quebec.

Confidential Negotiations

The initial discussions leading to the New Agreement between the Crees and the Province of Quebec were conducted in private, publicized only with the signing of an Agreement in Principle on October 23, 2001. At a time when the provincial newspapers were carrying weekly stories about the divisions between the Crees and Quebec, news of the Agreement in Principle came as a complete surprise to most people.

More startling yet was the news that the proposed New Agreement would have to include Cree consent to build another hydroelectric project in Eeyou Istchee. Only months earlier, the development plans of Hydro-Québec had run aground in Waskaganish when the General Assembly considering a proposed project decided against it. Now, the Crees were being asked to approve virtually the same project, which would divert the Rupert River. However, as more details of the Agreement in Principle came to light, it grew clear that the Crees had much to gain from the proposed New Agreement—much more than simple financial compensation.

The Eastmain-Rupert Diversion Project is, in fact, made up of two smaller projects (EM 1 and EM 1A) to be added to the existing La Grande Project. Construction of the EM 1 project will begin in 2002. It includes a dam with installed powerhouses and a reservoir (forebay) about 600 square kilometres (230 square miles) in size. The EM 1A part of the Eastmain-Rupert Diversion Project will be built at a later date, conditional on environmental approval.

This project will divert approximately 80 percent of the Rupert River's flow, measured at the diversion point, or about 50 percent if measured at the mouth of the river. The diversion will lead to additional flooding of about 220 square kilometres (85 square miles). To accommodate the additional water, another smaller dam and powerhouse (EM 1A) will be added near the EM 1 powerhouse.

The total Eastmain-Rupert Diversion Project will result in an increase to the energy output of the La Grande Project by about 11 or 12 terawatt hours. In comparison, the proposed Great Whale Project would have added about 14 terawatt hours of electrical energy and had reservoirs of about 3,300 square kilometres (1,270 square miles).

The confidentiality of the negotiations was rooted in political necessity. Since the completion of the La Grande Project, Phase I of the James Bay hydroelectric development project, the province and Hydro-Québec had been unsuccessful in moving ahead with Phase II. The province's attempts to implement both the Great Whale Project and the Nottaway, Broadback, and Rupert's Project had been stalled by Cree campaigns against them. This eventually led to the shelving of the Great Whale Project, for both political and economic reasons, during the lead-up to the Quebec sovereignty referendum.

Hydro-Québec had adopted a policy of dealing separately with each Cree community. Rather than conducting talks through a common Cree Nation negotiator, the provincial utility had tried to sell its development plans to the affected communities one-by-one. Many Crees saw this repugnant approach as "divide and conquer" colonialism.

In the spring of 2000, Hydro-Québec made a development proposal to the Waskaganish and Eastmain communities. It involved a diversion of the Rupert River into the Eastmain 1 forebay and construction of EM 1 and EM 1A. Hydro-Québec proposed that the Crees use a loan guarantee by the provincial utility to borrow funds to invest in the project. The Crees would then receive a percentage of the project's revenues, based on their percentage of ownership. They could use these proceeds to repay the loan, with excess revenues to be used however they wanted.

One of the problems with the 2000 proposal was that basic Cree resource rights were ignored—the Crees' own equity in the land was not recognized. Furthermore, the proposed profits were slim and the risk was high. Moreover, while the dam was being built, the Crees would still be in court with the Government of Quebec, battling over implementation of the James Bay and Northern Quebec Agreement. In a nutshell, Quebec would get its hydro project while the resolution of the fundamental problems of Cree development would once again get pushed into the background.

In July 2001, the Grand Council of the Crees called for a General Assembly in Waskaganish to discuss the proposal. Hydro-Québec's Vice-President, Thierry Vandal, attended to speak about the commercial opportunities and environmental impacts of the proposal. During the afternoon session, the dry technical proceedings were interrupted by a procession of elders and youth bringing a canoe into the room and placing it on the floor. Vandal was asked to sit in the canoe, which he did with great reluctance. The Crees then told him, "This is what it feels like to be in a canoe on dry land—we don't like it either." Hydro-Québec's efforts to divide and conquer were effectively ended, and their previous policy of corporation-to-First-Nation negotiations was dead.

After the breakdown of negotiations with Hydro-Québec at Waskaganish, it became apparent to Quebec Premier Bernard Landry and Ted Moses, Grand Chief of the Grand Council of the Crees, that new nation-to-nation approaches were needed if the two sides were going to resolve their differences. The two leaders met and laid out their fundamental principles and issues. Grand Chief Moses explained the Crees' position: the people needed housing, jobs, and a new approach to forestry—clear-cutting was erasing

Left to right: Matthew Coon Come, National Chief, Assembly of First Nations; Quebec Premier Bernard Landry; Ted Moses, Grand Chief, Grand Council of the Crees.

the traditional Cree way of life over vast areas. Premier Landry explained Quebec's desire to continue development of the north.

Each of the parties needed firm commitments from the other side that the decisions made by both parties would stand, and would not be easily reversed or changed afterwards. Each appointed two high-level representatives to discuss whether some resolution of their differences was possible. The Crees were represented by Abel Bosum, a past Chief of Oujé-Bougoumou, and Robert Mainville, a lawyer representing the Crees. Quebec was represented by Jean St. Gelais, Secretary General of the Government of Quebec, and Daniel Bienvenue, Deputy Secretary General of the Quebec Ministry of the Executive Council—the two highest level civil servants in the provincial government.

Both parties knew that discussions around community and resource development would be impossible if outside interest groups tried to interfere. For each outstanding issue, there would be a separate audience that might use public and/or legal pressures to influence the discussions. Forestry companies, mining companies, Hydro-Québec, the environmental lobby, consumer groups and others—all were touched by the issues. Even the federal government, a signatory to the 1975 treaty, might end up stalling discussions. Hence, the preliminary talks between the parties were held in private.

After two months of frank discussions, the parties came to an Agreement in Principle. It dealt primarily with Section 28 of the James Bay and Northern Quebec Agreement, which addresses government obligations for community and economic development. The Agreement in Principle stated that Quebec would transfer its implementation obligations for certain parts of Section 28 to the Grand Council of the Crees, giving them increased control over their own communities and economic development. The Crees would be funded with a long-term guaranteed source of revenues from resource development throughout the full extent of their traditional lands. Through this means, Cree rights embodied in the James Bay and Northern Quebec Agreement would be strengthened. In another 50 years, the Crees and the Province of Quebec would sit down once again to discuss their treaty commitments.

Before signing the Agreement in Principle and committing to further discussions, Grand Chief Moses had taken the proposal to the nine community chiefs and to the Deputy Grand Chief, Matthew Mukash. He asked them whether they would support further discussions, which they agreed to unanimously. After the October 23, 2001 public signing in Quebec City, the Grand Chief, Deputy Grand Chief, and community chiefs began the process of consulting the members of all nine Cree communities on the details of the proposed New Agreement. The people had the opportunity to consider the elements proposed in the Agreement in Principle. They could suggest changes to be brought forward during the negotiation of the final agreement, and the result would be presented for approval to the people at a future date.

The Cree leaders visited each of the nine communities. In addition, the Grand Chief met with Cree student groups in Montreal, Ottawa, and North Bay. Some took issue with the confidential nature of the discussions that had led to the October 23 signing. Once they understood the reasons for this and saw the true nature of the Agreement in Principle, however, most realized the crucial importance of the proposal to the future of the Cree people. There remained a small disaffected, but very vocal, group of Crees who strongly and publicly opposed the agreement with Quebec. Their biggest complaints were against the proposed partial diversion of the Rupert River.

Improving the Cree Way of Life

For most Crees, it is obvious that they must find new ways of creating jobs for their people. Hunting, fishing, and trapping will always be a major occupation for the Crees, and many of them will choose to pursue this as their way of life. Hunters still contribute significant quantities of nutritious and healthful food to their communities. But these important activities can no longer stand as the only Cree way of life. The Cree population has doubled in the past 25 years, and is likely to double again within the same time frame. Clearly, the Cree territory—developed or not—could never support such a large population of hunters.

Already, two of every three Crees are dependent on employment in the Cree School Board, the Cree Board of Health and Social Services, Cree local and regional governments, or the private sector. Many are unemployed: in some communities, as many as 40 percent of the people cannot find employment.

The Crees need jobs, good housing, good health care, and access to sustainable development. Although the 1975 Agreement guaranteed these rights and opportunities, the provincial and federal governments have not honoured their guarantees. Grand Chief Moses reminded his people, "For years, our rights were not respected; we could not benefit from the resources on our own lands. We depended on what government agreed to give. The result was unemployment, poverty, poor housing, and poor health."

Billy Diamond, a seasoned Cree negotiator and former Grand Chief, was at first concerned about the confidential nature of the negotiations, too. But after learning of the details of the proposed agreement, he agreed with those who had negotiated the deal. He stated:

> *Governments do not make these kinds of offers on a daily basis. The governments are serious about settling the issues with the Crees when they offer such an agreement and we will never again see this kind of offer. This is unprecedented and unparalleled in its magnitude. Think about it: a [premier] and a grand chief meet to discuss what it would take to solve the problems, and an offer is developed that includes most of what the Cree leadership has been putting forward for the last 26 years. Opportunities like this come once in a lifetime.*

Based on the feedback from the community consultations, more negotiations were held in December 2001, finalizing details of the New Agreement. The official signing date was set for February 7, 2002. The Grand Council of the Crees decided that each community should determine how it wanted to poll its residents regarding their decision on the Agreement. All nine communities opted for a referendum. To prepare for the referendums, the Cree leadership undertook another, even more extensive, round of community consultations—between December and February—to speak with and listen to the people prior to votes being cast.

In the end, a strong majority of the Cree people voted to accept the New Agreement. The referendums showed 70 percent of voting Crees were ready to embark on a new relationship with Quebec.

The Partial Diversion of a River

Perhaps the most contentious element of the New Agreement was giving Cree consent for the partial diversion of the Rupert River and construction of a power generating station and forebay on the Eastmain River. A few environmentalists and Crees were against any development that would affect any river.

After the Crees' tenacious fight to prevent the Great Whale Project from going ahead, and their more recent battles against the manner in which forestry has been managed on their traditional lands, some might ask why the Crees would now consent to more hydroelectric development. But the Cree Nation has never been against all development in its territory. Even during the fight to block the Great Whale Project, the Crees consented to the Troilus Mine near Mistissini and to two dams on the already developed La Grande River. What they have fought against is development that is too destructive of their land. And they have fought for the right to be involved in development, rather than subject to it.

Matthew Coon Come, former Grand Chief of the Crees and current National Chief of the Assembly of First Nations, summed it up best:

In the past, we have fought development when they wanted too much, when the projects they proposed were too large and destructive of the land. In Great Whale, they wanted to block three rivers, and put powerhouses on the Great Whale. In [Nottaway, Broadback, and Rupert's], they wanted to block another two large rivers and put the powerhouses on the Broadback River. They wanted seven rivers. I look at the Agreement before us, and I see that they want to block one river. This is progress.

Phase I of the James Bay hydroelectric project, the La Grande Project, flooded 13,500 square kilometres (5,212 square miles) of Cree land, affected four major rivers, and seriously damaged more than 30 family hunting territories. The proposed Great Whale and Nottaway, Broadback, and Rupert's projects would have involved seven major rivers, flooded 11,500 square kilometres (4,440 square miles) of land, and affected more than 50 traplines. In the New Agreement, by contrast, one major river would be partially diverted and two small rivers affected: the Rupert River would be reduced to a little more than half of its present flow at the mouth. In total, 959 square kilometres (370 square miles) of land will be flooded, affecting 11 traplines. Part of Grand Chief Ted Moses' own family hunting territory will be affected.

Additional agreements have been made to undertake remedial work to offset, as much as possible, the environmental effects of the new hydroelectric development. Most, if not all, of this work—and a large portion of the dam construction—will be done by the Crees themselves. This will create badly needed employment opportunities, and place design and management decisions with the people who are closest to the land. In addition, programs are being introduced that will make permanent jobs available to Crees as development is undertaken throughout the territory.

The New Agreement stipulates that Hydro-Québec will cancel the Nottaway, Broadback, and Rupert's Project, providing protection for these watersheds. By agreeing to a partial diversion of the Rupert River and some increased flooding, the Crees have ensured that two other large rivers will continue to flow and that over 7,500 square kilometres (2,895 square miles) of their traditional lands will be saved from flooding.

The very realistic Coon Come concluded: "If we do not sign, we can rest assured that the government will be back for the rivers and lakes. Will we win the next time?" Such realism is based on experience: in the early 1970s, the Crees waged a court battle to have the La Grande Project stopped and their rights recognized. While a superior court recognized their rights and found in their favour, a court of appeal overturned the decision. The project was built anyway.

Moses' opinion on the New Agreement is equally pragmatic:

There is a cost to the Crees. You can't want revenue from development and then not have any development. I have been fighting for jobs for our people, decent housing, and quality health services. The Agreement passes Quebec's responsibilities to the Crees and cuts the Cree government into the revenue stream created by the development already on the territory and that will be built in the future. In the past, these revenues have helped Quebec to grow; they will now begin to help us develop. The Crees assume management and control—for the first time we have some significant Cree control.

The Rupert River at Waskaganish

Waskaganish is my home. The river is in front of the community, and we used to swim there when I was young. I set my first net there. We all leave in our boats from the river's mouth when we go out into the Bay. In the fall we go to Notimeshanan [a traditional fishing site] and rebuild the wayapsinigan [a weir], where we catch ciscoes in dip nets. The river flows through the lands of Waskaganish, Nemaska, and Mistissini, where over 5,000 of our people live.

Our history is wrapped in the river. At the beginning of the last century, a crew of Waskaganish men took goods inland, and on a short trip back to the community their canoe overturned. Five of them died. This was a great tragedy for our people.

The river is part of us, ingrained in our souls—it has hurt us, it has fed us, and we live beside it. We need to allow future generations opportunities to prosper from rational development of the natural resources in Eeyou Istchee. The alternative is to watch as more resources are taken away from us to benefit others. Yes, our river will not be the same, but the benefits can finally come to our people.

Bill Namagoose
Executive Director of the
Grand Council of the Crees

A Landmark Agreement

Ever since the Quebec government's 1971 announcement of a proposed series of extensive hydroelectric projects within Eeyou Istchee, the Crees have struggled with the governments of Canada and Quebec for recognition as the rightful owners of the land, with a right to determine how it would be developed. At that time, the Province of Quebec announced plans to construct three hydro developments: the La Grande Project, the Great Whale Project, and the Nottaway, Broadback, and Rupert's Project. All told, the projects proposed to divert 10 rivers, flood 25,000 square kilometres (9,653 square miles) of land, and affect at least 70 traplines. Thirty-one years later, the Crees have made enormous strides in their battle to become involved in development decisions. Through the New Agreement, they have also saved several rivers and advanced toward their objective to be recognized as the owners of the land.

The New Agreement addresses human rights and social and economic development in Eeyou Istchee. It implements some of the most important recommendations of the Royal Commission on Aboriginal Peoples and the operational principles of self-determination called for by the United Nations Human Rights Committee under the International Covenant on Civil and Political Rights. It seems ironic, therefore, that the Royal Commission's sponsor, the Government of Canada, is not party to the Agreement. For the first time in Canada, a government and an Aboriginal people have made a joint commitment to implement one of the most essential elements of self-determination: the right of an Aboriginal people to benefit from the resources derived from their ancestral lands.

The New Agreement covers most, if not all, of the social, economic, and political issues raised earlier in this book. The 1975 James Bay and Northern Quebec Agreement remains in place and is unaffected by the New Agreement, except that the Government of Quebec has transferred its Section 28 obligations to the Crees. For the next 50 years, Quebec will provide the funds for the Crees to assume responsibility for implementing their own community and economic development, based on the following:

- *The Province of Quebec and the Crees will deal with one another on a nation-to-nation basis.*
- *The Crees will assume Quebec's obligations with respect to Cree communities and for economic development as set out in Section 28 of the James Bay and Northern Quebec Agreement, for a period of 50 years.*
- *Quebec will pay the Crees $24 million in 2002–03, $46 million in 2003–04, and $70 million in each of the following 48 years.*
- *Payments to the Crees will be indexed according to increases in the total value of mining, forestry, and hydroelectric production from the full extent of the Cree traditional territory.*
- *A number of outstanding lawsuits between Quebec and the Crees will be settled.*
- *A new regime will regulate forestry, to be implemented in co-operation with the Crees. Forestry planning will be at the level of family hunting territories, and Cree tallymen or ouchimaws will be allowed to protect critical areas of habitat.*
- *Quebec will support Cree involvement in future development of the region.*
- *The Crees will consent to the Eastmain/Rupert Diversion Project.*
- *Quebec will abandon the Nottaway, Broadback, and Rupert's Project.*
- *Quebec will create parks and protected areas in Eeyou Istchee, to be managed jointly by the Crees and the province.*

The New Agreement goes a long way toward our goals—not the whole distance, but a long way. No one ever gets everything they want in any negotiation. Quebec asks for Cree consent for two projects on the Eastmain and Rupert Rivers. Quebec sees the Cree Nation with resource rights over all of our territory .... We have come very far since 1974, when Quebec said we had no rights. So all of this effort has helped Quebec understand Cree rights.

Former Grand Chief Billy Diamond

Of course, there are those in the Cree camp and elsewhere who are cynical about the New Agreement. They say that the Crees and Quebec will never agree. But, perhaps it is the spirit with which the two traditional opponents entered into the new discussions that carried them through to an agreement to travel in the same canoe. Quebec appreciates that co-operation with the Crees is in the best interest of everyone. Any who might try to undermine the Crees' efforts to shape the way that development takes place in their territory will now face an even more powerful opponent.

A Nation-to-Nation Relationship

Non-Aboriginal Canadians might be puzzled by the New Agreement's reference to a "nation-to-nation" relationship between the Crees and Quebec. The province has twice attempted—and failed—to seek a mandate from Quebecers to recreate Quebec as a sovereign nation. However, this quest for sovereignty is predicated on the province's self-identification as a nation with the right to self-determination—not unlike the Crees' view of themselves. This concept of relationship is not new among Aboriginal groups, who have long insisted that their relationships with governments be based on nation-to-nation agreements.

It has always been clear to the Crees that, in a nation-to-nation relationship, neither nation subsumes the other. While respecting Quebec as a nation, nothing in the New Agreement prevents the Crees from maintaining their own international rights as a people and their own Cree Nation status within Canada and Quebec. The Crees continue to defend their right to make decisions about their own political status and relations with other peoples.

In negotiating the New Agreement, the Cree leadership was impressed by the willingness of Quebec to address the future and to build a new relationship based on mutual respect, co-operation, and partnership—a nation-to-nation relationship. When the Crees realized the many benefits they would gain from the New Agreement, they asked, with some suspicion, "What does Quebec gain?"

The simplicity of the answer—the opportunity for economic development and peace with the Crees—cannot be fully appreciated without a fuller understanding of the Crees' role in the province's most recent sovereignty referendum. The Crees' unfailing challenges to development initiatives imposed on their territory must also be considered, along with the numerous court cases they had launched against Quebec and Canada based on these governments' failure to implement the James Bay and Northern Quebec Agreement.

After the La Grande Project, Quebec's aspirations to further develop the hydroelectric potential of Eeyou Istchee were effectively stalled at every turn by the Crees. In the late 1980s and early 1990s, Quebec tried to advance Phase II of the James Bay hydroelectric development project (the Great Whale Project and the Nottaway, Broadback, and Rupert's Project). Through national and international campaigns against the development projects, the Crees proved to be such effective opponents that Premier Jacques Parizeau shelved the Great Whale Project in 1995. He thus hoped to rid the Parti Québécois of a significant political obstacle to its drive for secession. Instead of silencing the Crees, Premier Parizeau simply turned a page in Quebec history to find the Crees positioning themselves and their territory at the centre of a sovereignty referendum.

By 2001, the new Premier of Quebec, Bernard Landry, could see that the province's potential hydroelectric revenues would never be achieved without Cree co-operation. He opted for a new approach—one that marks an extraordinary evolution in the relations between a government and an Aboriginal people in Canada. At the ceremony to sign the New Agreement, Grand Chief Ted Moses said: "I want it to be clearly known that it is the imagination and the courage of Premier Landry that makes possible this fundamental change in historical direction."

Premier Landry's motivations are no secret. Increased hydroelectric revenues will be a critical factor in strengthening Quebec's economy. Indeed, some have said that the Crees are playing into the hands of the separatists, giving them exactly what they want and need to achieve an independence they might seek to impose upon the Crees. However, the New Agreement itself counters this position. Through it, Quebec will count the Crees in, not out, when making decisions about developments in their territory. The New Agreement even acknowledges the Crees' right of prior consent to proposed development on their lands.

This partially reverses some of the implications of the well-established government policy of extinguishment. Historically, treaties between Canadian governments and Aboriginal groups have required that Aboriginal peoples sign away their lands and resource rights forever. In the past, the Province of Quebec has also insisted that the Crees did not have rights to the resources of their lands. In negotiating the New Agreement, Premier Landry began to reverse this policy and showed a new respect for the rights of Aboriginal peoples—rights that have been acknowledged internationally. In 1999, for example, the United Nations ruled that Canadian Aboriginal title extinguishments are in violation of the Aboriginal right to self-determination.

Federal policy is still tied to the notion that Aboriginal peoples should be given a meagre payment to give up their right to benefit from the resources and economies of their lands—that they should be given a pittance to be shut off from their own economic resources—to become permanent dependants on government. This New Agreement with Quebec goes a long way toward the de facto reversal of the abhorrent concept of extinguishment.

Grand Chief Ted Moses
Speech given at the New Agreement signing ceremony

Building a nation-to-nation relationship required concessions from both Quebec and the Crees. When the two parties sat down at the negotiating table, between them sat the spectre of billions of dollars of litigation. The Crees had launched court actions against Quebec for failing to fulfill its treaty obligations under Section 28 of the 1975 James Bay and Northern Quebec Agreement. Under the New Agreement, the two parties settled 16 outstanding lawsuits out-of-court and reached further agreements about contentious mining, forestry, and hydroelectric issues.

By transferring the 1975 Agreement's Section 28 obligations to the Crees for implementation, the New Agreement eliminates a number of contentious issues, while confirming Quebec's duty to provide the necessary funds to carry out the work that is required. Quebec's transfer of responsibility marks a change in the traditionally paternalistic approach that governments have taken with Aboriginal peoples—an approach that once prompted governments to issue rations instead of family allowance money to Aboriginal people, believing that they should not be trusted with cash. The New Agreement turns away from this approach on a grand scale. While it is difficult to explain why it took so long for such a change to come about, it is nonetheless remarkable. The Province of Quebec is the first and only government in Canada to seek such a truly new relationship with Aboriginal peoples.

Sharing the Benefits of Development

The 1975 James Bay and Northern Quebec Agreement sets out Cree rights to continue their traditional way of life over the whole of their territory, and to become involved in development of these lands. However, according to that Agreement, all lands were transferred to the Province of Quebec and divided into three categories. Category 1 is Cree community land and falls under special federal and provincial legislation. Category 2 lands are exclusively for Cree hunting, fishing, and trapping. Category 3 is subject to Cree regimes on environmental protection and development. The Crees can control the extraction of minerals on Category 1 lands, because they control access, although the sub-surface nominally belongs to Quebec.

Under the New Agreement, Quebec will support Cree involvement in all future development throughout the full extent of Eeyou Istchee. Also, revenues paid to the Crees will be indexed to the value and volume of mining, forestry, and hydroelectric production from all three categories of land. This revenue sharing is in addition to the $70 million that Quebec will provide annually to implement its transferred Section 28 obligations. At last, the Crees will become beneficiaries of resource development throughout all of Eeyou Istchee.

Category 1 land:
5,542 square kilometres
(2,140 square miles)

Category 2 land:
62,155 square kilometres
(24,000 square miles)

Category 3 land:
277,157 square kilometres
(107,018 square miles)

Eeyou Istchee total:
344,854 square kilometres
(133,158 square miles)

A New Forestry Regime

In 1999, the Crees won an important decision in a court case on forestry, whereby Quebec Superior Court Judge Jean-Jacques Croteau instructed the Government of Quebec to amend its forestry legislation to be consistent with the Crees' rights under the James Bay and Northern Quebec Agreement. Two months after this visionary decision, which recognized the paramountcy of Aboriginal treaty rights, the Quebec Court of Appeal overturned Justice Croteau's decision and dismissed him from the case. Such were the fleeting victories of the Crees in the Canadian justice system, and this record was wearing thin with the Cree people.

For years, the Crees have been marginalized in their own territory by prohibitive conditions in the provincial Forestry Act. The New Agreement provides for a new regime to regulate forestry in Eeyou Istchee and to protect the Crees' traditional way of life. This regime will also be recognized in a new section of the 1975 James Bay and Northern Quebec Agreement.

Despite persistent but diminishing opposition from the forestry industry, the Province of Quebec has agreed that forestry management will now involve Aboriginal representation. The major provisions are as follows:

- *Forestry practice will be adapted to the Cree way of life by a Cree-Quebec Forestry Board.*
- *Plans for construction of forestry access roads will take Cree land use into account.*
- *Cree hunting territories will be designated as the basic forestry management units, which will ensure that traplines are not unduly affected by forestry operations.*
- *Clear-cutting will be restricted, with certain areas to be designated by Aboriginal people as closed to forestry operations for species protection, maintenance of biological diversity, harvesting of medicinal plants, and special cultural or traditional use.*
- *Cree ouchimaws, who have traditionally controlled access to the land, will be appointed as game wardens. They will assume new responsibilities as scientific advisers and managers of the forestry activities on their ancestral hunting grounds.*
- *The Cree Nation will be allocated an additional minimum of 350,000 cubic metres (457,800 cubic yards) of timber annually for their own forestry companies.*
- *Quebec will ensure that the Crees have a fair share of forestry contracts and employment.*

The New Agreement offers many opportunities for the Crees to enter into forestry ventures, setting the stage for the Cree Nation to capture the full potential of the forestry resources they possess.

Cree Identity—A People of the Land

Traditionally, the Crees have managed their land in an efficient and sustainable manner. They have been a practical people, with respectful and realistic practices and values that have evolved to ensure the Crees' long-term survival in an unforgiving landscape and climate. Like all peoples, the Crees do have a spiritual side. But some Crees have developed a romantic image of themselves as a people of inherently superior spirituality, connected to the land in mystical ways that preclude participation in development.

Bill Namagoose, Executive Director of the Grand Council of the Crees, says that these beliefs are not based on Cree ways. They are imported. He gives the example of the eagle and eagle feather, which in recent years have been broadly adopted by Aboriginal peoples as symbols of pride, strength, and spiritual power. "The eagle was not respected by the Crees in the past," Namagoose notes. "It was a scavenger bird and not liked by the hunters."

He believes that the spirituality movement that has evolved among North American Native groups in the past few decades is often not far removed from the old "noble savage" stereotype developed in the European-derived North American societies. "It is a myth," Namagoose says, "that we can only walk softly on the land and not extract anything for economic benefit. This kind of thinking only supports government policies that refuse us ownership of our land. It gives an excuse to others to do as they please on the land. Projects are not always acceptable, but by rejecting all development we give others the excuse to exclude us from ownership and benefit."

Namagoose refers to a 1999 Supreme Court of Canada decision in the case of Donald Marshall Jr., a Mi'kmaq Indian who was charged with fishing in violation of federal fishery regulations. The court found that Marshall had a right of access to fishing resources for the purpose of earning a "moderate living." A moderate living was defined by the court as acquiring enough resources for "food, clothing and housing, supplemented by a few amenities." While supporting Marshall's right to fish, Namagoose challenges government policies and court judgments that seek to restrict entrepreneurial enterprises by Aboriginal peoples. "We have a right as a nation to develop natural resources, to generate wealth, and to develop our communities. No agreement will solve all of our problems forever—nothing could. However, [the New Agreement] gives us the chance of becoming, once again, the major economic and governmental force on Eeyou Istchee, as the Eeyouch always were in the past."

The Challenge Ahead

The signing of the New Agreement has placed broad new responsibilities on the Crees. Ask them if they are ready to take on the complex work of community and economic development for the next 50 years, and the Crees will reply that this is what they have always fought for. With the Agreement in Principle on the table, the Crees quickly organized themselves to address the possibilities of the future.

In December 2001, in anticipation of confirming the agreement, Billy Diamond organized a meeting of Cree companies to discuss how they might best work together to take advantage of the New Agreement. In answer, the Eeyou Istchee Consortium was

formed: a non-profit organization with a mandate to ensure fair and equitable distribution of jobs and contracts among the Cree labour force and businesses. The Consortium will encourage networking and mutual co-operation among Cree businesses and service organizations. Its board will include a representative from each of the nine communities.

Another organization, the Cree Development Corporation, was created by the New Agreement and will operate as an autonomous corporation with a board comprising a majority of Cree directors. This corporation has a mandate to oversee and facilitate economic development in Eeyou Istchee. It will address such important issues as job creation, the start-up of Cree businesses, and partnerships with non-Cree companies.

The Crees acknowledge that there is a lack of professional and technical expertise among their own people at present—they need more people with financial and business training—but their people have plenty of hands on business experience and a will to effect change. More and more Crees are completing advanced education and becoming doctors, lawyers, teachers, social workers, and other professionals. The chance to participate more fully in their own community development will be an incentive to young Crees, who can now imagine viable employment opportunities in the territory and in their own communities. With the New Agreement, the Crees can re-occupy their traditional territory in new ways by participating in the development of their lands.

As a people, the Crees have faced what other Aboriginal peoples also face—forced assimilation brought on by dispossession of their lands and the attendant poverty and social disintegration that inevitably follow. Their alternative has been to evolve in response to a changing world, to fight for recognition of their rights, and to win inclusion in access to the wealth of their land.

Every society, Aboriginal or non-Aboriginal, must be willing to accommodate various groups if any are to have a sustainable future. The world is becoming more interdependent, not less so. Co-existence and co-operation are paths to survival: isolation does not have a future.

Confronted with this reality, the Crees have freely chosen to participate in developing their own future. For other Aboriginal peoples, there is no choice—their right to benefit from the resources of their land continues to be denied, in violation of their human rights. The land that has sustained them as nations for thousands of years is now benefiting others, while their own people are forced to leave or remain in poverty, dependent on government. They must fight for their rights, as the Crees continue to do in Eeyou Istchee.

The signing of the 1975 Agreement marked the beginning of a new era for the James Bay Crees. By standing united as communities and as Cree citizens, they have remained committed to their own concept of nationhood. Their leaders have been strong and wise political opponents who have worked tenaciously to protect Cree rights. That will not change under the New Agreement with Quebec.

I think that the children in the future will benefit from the New Agreement, just as we have benefited from the James Bay [and Northern Quebec] Agreement. At first, I didn't like it. But when I think about my children and grandchildren—some of them do not have work. Many young people do not have work, even though they went to school. Some of these people, when they see that the [New] Agreement is signed, will go back to school to get the qualifications with the new funding, so that they will be able to find work. I really like the look of this agreement that will last for 50 years.

Luke Tent
Hunter/Trapper

I believe that the choice we have made is best, both for the Cree people and for Eeyou Istchee, the land. When the day comes that there is full respect for the human rights of all Indigenous peoples, others will also be able to make this choice for a more sustainable future.

Grand Chief Ted Moses

Cree Lives and Voices

Travelling Among the Crees

Perhaps the richest elements of this book arise from the voices of the Crees themselves. The fleeting insight we are able to gain into their culture, values, and lifestyle serves to enrich our understanding of, and commands our respect for, this vibrant, proud, and independent people. To gather these interviews required a specialized set of skills. Boyce Richardson, a respected journalist among the Crees, spent part of the summer of 1999 visiting Cree villages in search of people to interview. As readers will agree, Boyce's efforts were successful.

First visiting Mistissini in 1969, Boyce was the first mainstream journalist in Canada to cover the situation of the James Bay Crees. He had no idea then that his life would undergo a dramatic transformation that would forever connect him with the Cree people.

His first impressions were of a despondent people that were rapidly being transformed into an impoverished, dispossessed group pushed to the brink of their endurance. Gradually, however, Boyce was led on a remarkable journey through which he discovered the beauty, harmony, and strength that the Crees found in their most natural habitat, the bush. These were not the unsophisticated, dependent people the government insisted they were. Quite the contrary, the Crees showed him the unmatched expertise they had in coexisting with their environment. He found that their technical skills in hunting, clothing production, and basic survival were unsurpassed, and their knowledge of animal behaviour exceeded that of most scientists. While bush life was by no means without risk and discomfort at times, the Crees knew intimately what the land could offer and how to make the best of its resources—and they faced its challenges with fortitude and humour.

Just as he had fallen, almost by accident, into his contact with the Crees, so Boyce fell into making films. His films, *Job's Garden* and *Cree Hunters of Mistassini*, portray the Crees at ease in their world, comfortable in their knowledge and skills, and having an inherent respect for the land and its resources. An updated version of the first film, entitled *Flooding Job's Garden*, looks more closely at the changes that the Crees have undergone in response to the onslaught that was the James Bay hydro project.

Accompanying Boyce on his 1999 summer trip was his son, Thom, a talented writer and film producer from Montreal. Together, the two men visited the Cree communities and interviewed an impressive 45 people in 10 days. Many doors were readily opened to them due largely to the friendships Boyce has developed over the years, the recognition and respect he has gained for his work, and the role he has played letting the world know about the James Bay Crees.

A Famous Cree Trapping Family

Sam and Nancy Blacksmith became one of the most famous Cree hunting teams through a 1974 National Film Board film, *Cree Hunters of Mistassini*, which was shot on Sam's hunting territory, well inland and north of the Eastmain River. It was the first time a Cree hunter of James Bay had ever agreed to have his hunting life filmed, and audiences were spellbound by the staggering expertise the hunters revealed so simply as they went about their daily lives in the bush.

The film won international awards, was seen in countries throughout the world, and has been one of the most-screened movies about Aboriginal people ever made in Canada.

In the 1970s, Sam Blacksmith was a handsome, cheerful, indomitable figure, wonderfully expert in the multitude of tasks that fall to a Cree hunter. His simple philosophy, so simply expressed—"All seasons are good" and "No one can really own the land, because eventually everyone dies"—endeared him to people in many countries.

At the age of 83, he and his wife, Nancy, who have been married for 51 years, still love to go into the bush; they are unhappy when confined to the village of Nemaska, where their daughter Daisy now lives. "When he has to stay in the village, he doesn't say much around the house, and by the end of a week he stops talking to anybody," said Daisy. "When he's out in his bush camp, 25 kilometres from Nemaska, he's his usual cheerful self."

We found this wonderful couple, looking scarcely a day older than they did 25 years ago, squatting on the spruce boughs on the floor of their teepee beside a calm lake, accompanied by Abraham Mianscum, now 32, who was a small boy when the film was made. He is the son of another Mistassini hunter, Francois Mianscum, but in a fashion that is quite common among the Crees, Sam and Nancy have brought him up; he is slated to take over Sam's land when the time comes.

Sam Blacksmith, 83
Hunter

My father taught me many good things about the land. He lived off the land and he taught me the same. Then I became independent and I started to live on my own, following those teachings from my father—that's how I live today. They were good teachings. When my father was not able to continue living off the land, I was able to help him. Now I am older I want to tell you that I'm not able to do what I used to be able to do on the land. But I still try to do as much as I can for myself, and I have Abraham to assist me.

When my father lived off the land, there was no food from the White man. Our food came from the land. I was born not too far from here, on Tommy Neeposh's trapline. The land where we were when the film was made, Lac Tréfart, had been passed on to the elder who gave it to me, so it is my land now. That is where I still hunt today, and my cabin is there. That is where I went last fall. I will give the land to Abraham [Mianscum] when I am gone.

From what I can see, the change in my land since the hydro project was built is that the beaver has not been there for at least five years. The trees are not there for the beaver to feed on. Where the road is, there are not as many animals as used to be there. Like the rabbit, the partridge, we don't see as many. There were no moose nearby; they were further out and they don't come as close.

They built a temporary road that was acceptable to go to the trapline. But now that they've finished what they are working on, that road is no longer there. I'm not happy with how the changes have affected my land. The fish have been destroyed by the water that came up from the temporary road. From all the land that is being destroyed, the fish are all being contaminated. Now we have to go further out to the lake to get food fish. They don't taste as good as they used to.

It has been hard to live off the land during my life, especially when I didn't have access to White man's food supplies. I used to work during the spring; I would travel at least five days walking, just to get to the post to get my supplies. That was hard for me. That's how it was in those days. I still live off the land and I try not to make it hard for others. Abraham is a good hunter; he knows everything there is to know. The only thing Abraham is missing now is that he doesn't want to get married.

They have destroyed a lot out on the land. They have destroyed Charlie Etapp's trapline. They have destroyed everything. When there was an Agreement, we were told that there was going to be help for us. Now I see that today we do receive money, but the money we receive goes back—it doesn't stay with us, it goes back. As you can see, we now live in a house. The money goes to the cost of the house. We were told when we had an Agreement we were going to get help, but many people ask, "How are we being helped?" It is very expensive to go and buy your goods, what you need, supplies, what you use. It is very expensive today.

I find that the people who are building these dams, they do not listen to us. They don't listen to what we have to say, even though we are talking. It's like they have heads like rocks.

There are people always concerned for what is happening to the land. We also have our youth, the generation of young people—they will go out on the land. But when I go out to my trapline it is very costly for me. I have to go by plane, which is very expensive.

Abraham Mianscum, 32
Hunter

My grandfather, Sam Blacksmith, who I love very dearly, has taught me to trap and hunt as a way of life, so when he told me that he was going to pass the land to me, I take it with honour and respect. Right now they are getting old, and I am not able to leave them out there alone for a long time by themselves. They worry about me when I am out there alone on the land.

When I am out there alone, I think of my grandfather, of when he was able to come with me, when we used to be able to walk together. I think about him when I see the land where we used to go. But now he is not able to do that.

Now today, it is very expensive just to go out here on the land. To pay for all your costs, that's the way it is now. To go over there and then to come back again, and pay all the costs. I work during the summer to make my money. So because of that, it has been on the Income Security Program. But this summer I was not able to find employment. I wanted to work for Hydro-Québec but they wouldn't hire me.

Usually if I go to our trapline by ski-doo in the winter, the longest time I am alone is one month. It takes me five hours to get there. We still have to be very careful, when we are alone. You learn by your mistakes. In the past two falls there was not as much game as there used to be before. It's getting more and more like that.

The land that my grandfather has passed on to me, I have now found people who will come and live with me: my brothers from Mistissini. I've got five brothers and two sisters.

Traditional Cree Women

The role of these remarkable women was vital to the success of the Cree hunting culture.

Cree women who grew up in the traditional life established an important position for themselves in Cree society. The range of their abilities was remarkable. They were tough, able to keep up with their men as they tramped the vast boreal forest in search of game, many of them giving birth in the hunting camps and helping other women through their births; they were expert in keeping the camps clean and sweet-smelling. In addition to dealing with the children and the camps, they processed all the meat and furs that were brought into camp.

It was said, 20 or 30 years ago, that the furs that came out of the Cree camps of James Bay were the best in the world. This would have been largely due to the expertise of these remarkable women in skinning the carcasses, stretching and drying the pelts, and preparing them for market. These women were also expert in sewing moccasins, fur and skin clothing and bedding, and making snowshoes.

All of the women who tell their stories here appear to have loved the solitude and the purity of the environment in which they raised their families. Although they could not be called liberated women in the modern sense of the term, anyone who has ever interviewed a Cree hunting elder realizes that Cree women were not shrinking violets. Usually while a hunter is being interviewed, his wife is hanging around nearby, muttering in Cree, telling her husband what to say or sitting by his side, perhaps cleaning fish, murmuring non-stop in Cree to ensure that her husband is telling it just right.

They were essential partners with their husbands and teachers for their children.

Many of these remarkable women now live in the Cree villages but their real home is in the bush, where they still go to live for months in a teepee, in the world they know, love, and have mastered.

In these interviews, women tell of lives that most Canadians could scarcely imagine: of the constant struggle to feed their families, of occasionally starving, of watching the gradual breakdown of the culture that they sustained (though they show faith in and hope for their young leaders).

Helen Mianscum
Oujé-Bougoumou

Helen Mianscum still forms half of a hunting and trapping team with her husband, John. They spend most of their time on the family grounds, south of the main road to Chibougamau, not far from the Chapais-Chibougamau airport. We caught up with her one Sunday afternoon in a cabin on this land. While her husband was reluctant to be interviewed, Helen talked freely, and with gusto, about her life as a hunter's wife.

When we went into the bush in the fall, and during the winter months, we used to make a tent frame. We'd just take the bark off the tree to use as insulation. We used moss as part of the insulation, and it made a very comfortable house. I had one daughter born in the bush. The midwife was an old lady who was in our camp. That daughter now lives in Chibougamau and works in the clinic with a dentist. Even when I gave birth in Mistissini, there were no medical facilities or doctors.

In the traditional days, when there were no vehicles on the road, there was not a lot of dust blown up into the moss, so the moss was good as a diaper. But now there's just too much gravel and dust on that moss, so it's not that good anymore.

Some of the roles that I had in the bush camp included: I had to keep the spruce boughs fresh; whenever we needed water I would go and fetch it; I would take the firewood inside; whenever a kill was made I had to prepare all the food; I had to prepare the moosehide, all the beaver pelts, and everything else that needed to be prepared; I also made moccasins and I continue to do it.

I still continue to go out today and I still enjoy it. We usually go out in September, and come back in about May after the goose break. All the kids that are not in school come with us, but the kids in school, we leave them there.

This is my traditional hunting territory. We still bring in beavers. He [her husband, John] still hunts pretty much everything that he used to hunt. People weren't as mobile back then and it was much better when we were more in one place. Nowadays, people keep moving all over the place. Once in a while, people would get together for a short time. But mostly we were in small groups. Only our immediate family was there. We always went to our own land.

Yes, I still love this life, but I liked the old, more traditional days better.

We learned to respect the animals. Sometimes today you'll see a dog eating the bone of an animal. In the traditional days, we wouldn't allow that to happen. It was believed that if you did that, you wouldn't be able to kill the animals. You wouldn't be able to survive. We showed respect for the animals after we killed them.

Those youth who were raised in the bush, they want to return to the bush, but those who weren't raised in the bush, they seem to not value the bush life as much as those that were raised in the bush.

Evadne Gunner, 73
Mistissini

Evadne Gunner has been for many years a pillar of the Mistissini community, a talkative, competent woman whose knowledge of the bush life is unexcelled. In 1974, when the Quebec government offered to buy Cree land in order to build hydro dams, hunters left the forest in the middle of winter, for the first time ever, to come to Mistissini to consider the offer: one after the other, the elders rose to warn that they could not exchange their land for money. Evadne made a remarkable speech (part of which was recorded in a National Film Board film, *Our Land Is Our Life*) in which she talked of the joy of bearing her children in the bush, and the difference this birthplace made in the child's perception of life. Memories of childhood hardships she suffered are strong in her still-active mind.

My dad was a hunter and an Anglican minister. I think I had only two brothers. I don't remember how many we had. Our family hunting territory was at Chibougamau. That's where my father brought me up and my sister. When my mother died, my sister was only about four years old. She's still alive around here somewhere; there's only the two of us left. After my mother died, my sister didn't understand what was going on in my family. She used to cry, all the time, "Mama, Mama." But her mother was gone. My father was hurt because she was calling her mother all the time.

Eventually, my dad brought us over here to another of his brothers and his family, people we used to go to live with in the bush. This lady is still alive. We still call her Mama, because she was so good to us. She and her husband are still alive and I always say to them whenever I see them, "Hello, Dad," and he says, "Hello, my daughter." "Hello, Mama." That's how I can say that, because they used to be so good to us. One time I saw her and hugged her with my arms, kissed her, and I said, "I love you, Mama." She said to someone, "Both these two women still call me Mama." And she told this person about all the troubles that happened to us and how we came to call her Mama because she was treating us just like our mother.

I would carry my little baby on the toboggan. I'd wrap him up in all the blankets. Then we used to have a little lunch somewhere. If we wanted a drink or were hungry I'd make a little fire for lunch. Then we'd keep on going.

I went to school when I was about 11 or 12. Chapleau was a residential school. Only me but not my sister. My brother didn't want to let every one of us go, so he kept my sister home. My sister used to always say that she should go to school.

I was 20 when I got married to a hunter. Right away we went into the bush. It was springtime, all the water was open. I had a little boy, he was born in the bush. I was okay after. I had to learn from the other people how to operate the camp. I didn't have to ask them but I had to use my eyes. Maybe sometimes if I didn't know anything, I would ask them. Cleaning up the tent, go getting the spruce boughs, doing my sewing; sometimes I would go with my husband when he went to the beaver traps.

A long time ago, when I was a child, when my mother was still alive, we used to have a hard time. We didn't even have any tea or sugar, a little bit of flour, a little bit of lard. My father used to make tea out of some kind of leaves in the bush. He used to gather a whole bunch of them and it used to taste just like tea. They said that was medicine, those leaves. If you don't feel good in your body or in your stomach, those leaves can help you. Like, if you take painkillers, those leaves are something like that. Sometimes, when my brother was kind of falling down, doing this or that, he asked somebody to cut the vein. That was the medicine. I got lots of cuts in my hand. When you don't feel good, you feel down and you don't feel like doing this or that, you're so weak and you want to lie down—if you take a little bit of your blood, it helps you for a long time. You don't need any medicine, just that. That's what my husband used to do to me when I didn't feel good. He'd say that maybe I had too much blood.

In the olden days, as far as I can remember, the people so liked living with each other. Like men together, working in the bush, hunting. After about two or three days, they'd come back and they'd bring some meat—beaver, rabbit, moose, partridges. We would share it with every family. That's all we had, and some bannock and lard, sugar, tea, coffee. That's all, nothing else. No canned food, nothing. When I was only about four or five years old, we were starving—we didn't have anything to eat. The little ones, they didn't understand what was going on. They'd ask their mothers, "Do you have some bannock or some partridges?" "No, we don't have nothing." That was the hardest time I remember. My sister would cry for my mother. And she would say, "That's why we don't have anything

We had three families that used to live in a big teepee together. In the middle, we used to have three stoves. We never quarreled because we liked living with each other.

to eat, because Mama left us." My mother died in the bush, in Chibougamau. That's where we buried her.

At that time, we had some but not very many beaver. It was only lynx and those little animals, like muskrat. Sometimes when we were hungry we used to eat a lot of bannock. The animals we liked best were beaver and some moose meat. Putting it on a stick over the fire. I always tell my grandchildren when I see some of them eating hamburgers, baloney, "My goodness, you eat like White people." They would say, "Granny, why do you say this?" I'd say, "When I was a kid your age, I never used to eat like this." "Well, what did you eat?" they would ask. "Just bannock." Sometimes we used to have sugar, and—you won't believe this if you haven't seen it—you know the rabbit's guts, we used to tie them together and hang them up. It used to get all dried up, and after, when it's all dried, they used to cut it open and they'd put some sugar in there and we used to eat it like that. The kids used to like that.

My father became minister because they needed a minister here. Some people used to have a little service at their tent but we never used to have a church. I still remember this old man who asked Bishop Clark if he could find a minister for here. He told him all about the people here and what they do and that we had no church, no houses, only tents. Anybody can pray and have a little service at the tents. And that bishop came here. There was an old man, George Iserhoff, who would go around to all the tents. But after he passed away, that is when they picked my dad. That's when they built the church. A log house, of course, because they didn't have boards.

We used to leave for the bush sometime in September and we'd come back only in June. We'd stay in the bush all these months. It was a pretty hard life. I wish you could try that. We were happy.

I had most of my children in the bush. I lost the only one born in a hospital, in Amos, when she was a baby. In the bush, we used to have a woman who would help with the birth. I had eight children in total. I used to always tell the young women when they have babies, "Why don't you stay at home and have your baby at home? Look at me, you see all the tall boys I have and they were all born in the bush. You could do the same thing." When I'm pregnant and ready to have my baby, I'm in the bush all the time. They are too scared to do that anymore. They don't know what's going to happen to them. Now they cry from the pain, I guess.

White men wanted to come in and destroy the place, and if we had said, "Yes, you can do this," everything would be gone. Living in a big city like Montreal, everything would be like that—a big, big town in the middle of an Indian's hunting ground. If we had said, "Yes, you can do whatever you like," you wouldn't be able to see all those trees across there [indicates trees on other side of inlet], all this would be gone. We would just see a big truck passing by. But even behind those trees there, they are cutting all the trees. White people are going to eat all those trees.

Yeah, some of the young people who did the negotiating did a good job, but some of them are too happy to have money. That's the trouble. They drink with their money. Even if their mother and daddy tell them not to do that. You can see a whole lot of teenagers walking around here drunk.

There's one boy here who's gone. He made a big damage to another boy, so he's gone. The boy I adopted, I always talk to him about that. He's working here, and I told him, "Don't be like your friend, he's gone." He's in jail and they don't know when they are going to let him go.

Hattie Moses, 79
Eastmain

Hattie and Willie Moses are quintessential Cree elders, better known perhaps than most because they are the parents of Cree Grand Chief Dr. Ted Moses, who has made a name for himself globally as the Cree ambassador to the United Nations. Hattie's family was described in a University of Saskatchewan citation as "an accomplished model for Aboriginal families" in Canada. Hattie was still full of vigour when we met her in 1999, and talked freely to us about her life.

My role as a woman in the hunting camp was to take care of the children and provide firewood for the family. The ladies that I learned from, they always taught me to have more than enough firewood. There was more to it than that, of course. I also had to look after the children because most of the time, my husband was away hunting. I was always taught to keep the place clean where I kept my children. Also I cooked and fetched the water. I was always there at the end of the day, preparing the food for my husband whenever he came back from hunting. I was also the one who skinned, cleaned, and dried everything.

Sometimes I would leave my kids in the teepee and go out all day to get the firewood.

All of my kids grew up in the bush with us. Including Dr. Ted Moses. Some of my kids were born in the bush. It takes a very strong woman to bring up a child in the bush. At this time of the year [early September], I used to start collecting the moss for my diaper supply so I would have enough for the winter. I'm an expert in that. I know which moss to use and which one not to use. The diapers they use today are not that good. The kids get a rash. I did an experiment recently where I let a kid with a rash wear moss diapers, and after that the rash was gone.

We were always taught that whenever we had the time, we should go hunting. That way, we provided enough of the things that we needed.

I never saw starvation but I've heard about it. There are many stories. My husband was a good hunter. But as I was growing up there were some very hard times when we didn't have anything to eat. My dad was getting old and couldn't provide enough food. The only reason we were fortunate to have food was that the women were also good hunters and we got the small animals. I feel fortunate that I never experienced any starvation. When I grew up, we were always told that our fathers would teach us how to hunt the small animals, and my father taught me that.

Sometimes we had rabbit here and then sometimes it seems like they vanished. It's the same thing with the moose. When I was a kid, I saw my father kill a moose, and after that I didn't see any moose being killed until I got married, 20 years later. It's like that with animals. Sometimes they are there but sometimes they go elsewhere. When they eat, you know where they eat but sometimes there is not enough food for the animals and they go elsewhere. But they always come back after the food has grown back.

I always did look forward to the goose hunting. Going back inland for the fall—I always looked forward to that. It was the old men who would decide when we'd go. They were the boss for the family and had to make all the decisions. I always looked forward to going back to the bush.

But now we can't go back to the bush. It's not something to look forward to now, going back to the bush, because of the destruction left behind by Hydro-Québec.

I had seven children and four of them are alive today. There's Bella [Petawabano] who lives in Mistissini; Ted, Joe, and Laura. All of my kids, including Ted, they all used the moss diapers. I never used the ones from the store on them. I have nine grandchildren. But I don't have any idea how they are doing because I usually see them only in the summertime when they are off from school. I encourage them to pursue their education because it's a way for them to make a living in the future. I'm proud of them, and of the way they are pursuing their education.

The Fiddlers of James Bay

Over the millennia, the Crees of James Bay have developed a rich culture that has been transferred orally from generation to generation. The Crees have adopted the best from the cultures that they have come into contact with, and from the Europeans they have taken on the steel trap and fiddling. The fiddle came straight from the Orkney Islands to James Bay, thanks to the Hudson's Bay Company.

From the early 1700s, the Hudson's Bay Company recruited workers from the Orkney Islands, which are north of mainland Scotland, to staff the outposts in James Bay. The islanders were relatively impoverished at the time and, to the Canadian recruiters, James Bay must have appeared as forbidding an environment as the islands. Many Orcadians jumped at the idea of gaining fame, and perhaps fortune, in the service of the Company. By the 1800s, the Orcadians made up 80 percent of the Hudson's Bay Company workers in what was then known as "Rupert's Land."

Not willing to sacrifice their lives to a monastic existence, and not sure whether they wanted to return home, many took Cree women as "country wives"—as they were referred to at the time—and raised families. These children were raised as Crees, with little emphasis placed upon their Scottish heritage. Most of the Orcadians returned home eventually. However, several elements of the Orkney culture became deeply woven into the cultural fabric of Cree life, including the presence of tartan blankets, tam-o'-shanters, the taking of tea and bannock, and the adoption of words such as bilessis, bayeechis, and wescot (braces, breeches, and waistcoat) into the Cree language. Notably, the first school

A 1980 National Film Board of Canada video, The Fiddlers of James Bay, *describes the odyssey of two of the best Cree fiddlers from James Bay. Ray Spencer and Bob McLeod accepted an invitation to travel to the Orkney Islands to play their fiddle music with an Orcadian orchestra.*

Neither man had ever been outside Canada, or even outside the James Bay area. The trip was a success, although the blending of the music proved difficult. There was no time before their joint perfomance to rehearse, and even the two Cree fiddlers had never played together before. Their reception by the orchestra members and audience was warm and enthusiastic, however, and the two groups were able to put on an impressive performance before the end of their short trip.

that taught in the Cree language was established in the 19th century in the Orkney Islands, for the returning families.

One of the most enduring influences of the Orcadians, however, was their music. Their love of fiddle music travelled with them across the 7,000 km (4,350 miles) from the Orkney Islands to James Bay. They brought fiddles with them, and the Crees carried these portable, durable instruments with them out to the traplines. While traditional Cree music comprised songs and drumming, the Crees picked up new tunes from the Orcadians and improvised on them. The Orcadians, Crees, and "Orcadiancrees" spent many an evening sitting around the fire drinking tea, eating bannock, and playing songs into the wee hours of the morning.

As economic conditions gradually improved in the Orkney Islands, the flow of Orcadians slowed and then stopped. The last ship sailed to James Bay in 1891. The music, however, survived and was passed down from generation to generation of Cree fiddlers. Today, some of the songs played at Cree dances have not been heard in the Orkney Islands for over 100 years. And on New Year's Eve, Cree fiddlers in James Bay continue the old Scottish tradition of going door to door, entertaining neighbours and bringing in the New Year with an old twist.

A Blast From the Past, James Bay Style

(From The Nation *magazine December 4, 1998,*
by William Nicholls)

James Cheechoo, a Cree from Moose Factory [Ontario], has just released his first music CD at 68. Cheechoo is of the old school, a self-taught fiddler who has been performing for the last 55 years, longer than most people have been married, though he's certainly played more than one wedding. He is one of the last fiddlers to remember the "old style" playing before guitars were introduced as back-up for the fiddle.

Cheechoo said his father remembered going about 40 miles out in the "Bay" to Charleton Island. "There was a depot for the HBC there," said Cheechoo. He said his father told him a lot of Crees would go there during the summer to watch the "three-masters" coming in. According to Cheechoo, it took about 14 days to unload the three-mast ships. "Scotsmen and Irishmen would come in the ships and they would be playing music all the way in to the warehouse," said Cheechoo, remembering his father's stories.

"They had a lot of fun dancing and playing the music. Some of these songs on this CD are from this time," said Cheechoo. Indeed, the name of the CD, Shay Chee Man, refers to those who came in on the ships to Canada to "bring those tunes to us," said Cheechoo.

The Nation: You're from the Moose Factory people?

> Yes, but when I speak Cree I speak the Cree language of Eastmain. That's where I was born. My father worked over there until he got his old age pension and moved back to Moose Factory. I moved back with him in 1960.

I see you're a self-taught fiddler. Do you read music?

> I don't read the notes of music. I just learned where I hear the music. I hear music and I can play it.

This album has 10 songs. These are all traditional dances?

> Yes, I do these things. These are history songs, very old songs. Nobody plays them now. They only want to play the new music. Everybody wants to play the new music.
>
> I brought these up because I heard some Indian people saying they want to bring up something that's old so young people can see and hear it.
>
> The Indians, what they were using a long time ago, they were dancing. I remember back in 1944, the first time that I was playing the fiddle in square dancing, it would start at 8 in the evening and finish at 5:30 or 6 in the morning. That's how long they used to dance. Of course they used to rest for about 15 minutes and they dance again. Other people used to play fiddle like I did.

So you're looking at this album as a way of preserving Cree history for the youth and future generations?

> Yes.

Are you teaching anyone the fiddle?

No, I never taught anyone. I just want to pass on the fiddle so people can hear it. The new fiddlers can give it a try if they want to carry on the old-time fiddle music. I know some places they have never heard this type of fiddle music. Especially at Chisasibi, I went in there last summer and they said there's some rabbit dancing in that music. They didn't know how the rabbit dance went.

The rabbit dance has two lines. One's a ladies' line and the other is the men's line. One partner has to chase his partner around these lines until he catches her. That's how the rabbit dance goes. Then it's the next couple and the next after that until all is finished. Sometimes the ladies take a little while to be caught. They run around the people who are sitting watching. It's a lot of fun.

Also there's a kissing dance. The kissing dance used to be the very last dance they would have at these dances. It was to say goodbye to people. They use a kerchief. It can be a lady or a man who starts first. If it's a man he dances around in a circle, he may have an eye on somebody. He goes and kisses the lady wherever they are sitting. He gives her the kerchief. She dances around and kisses a man. They dance around in a circle following each other until the last lady. She goes up and kisses the fiddler. He goes with his fiddle into the centre of the circle. Everyone's still going around and they all join hands because the fiddler has been kissed. The fiddler's in the centre of the ring. He chooses what lady he's going to kiss. He goes outside the circle and the lady goes to the middle. She kisses someone else and leaves the circle to sit down. The circle gets smaller as this goes on until there's only two left. That's the kissing dance. That's how that works. It finishes up the party.

You're thinking of another CD?

Yes, I can put in another five old traditional and five modern songs. I'd like to have people hear them. To hear what was going on a long time ago. This is so they cannot forget this music. That's very old. I can bring the skin drum too.

A long time ago there was no guitar. There was only the skin drum that was used, it was good. It was like a guitar sound with almost bass, it sounds real good. I remember hearing the sound from my house a long time ago when I would go outside. I could hear the dance going even though it was quite a ways away. That's how loud it was and it was good.

I noticed you have your wife playing on this CD too.

Yeah, my wife is playing the spoons. She has played with me a long time when she feels like it. She plays very good. She's got some wooden spoons from her sister. They're attached together. That's how they are, those spoons.

Chisasibi Artist

Margaret Orr, 37

Margaret Orr is a young Cree woman who has doggedly pursued a career as a visual artist, is beginning to make a name for herself. Her father was a Scotsman who came over to work for the Hudson's Bay Company, fell in love with Gracie Orr of Chisasibi, and married her. Margaret was born in Prince Albert, Saskatchewan, after her father "dragged my mom out there because he got a job." Later, the family moved back to Moose Factory, Ontario, where her father was a supervisor at the residential school.

After high school I came and lived in the bush and picked up on stuff. From many different people: my mom, my grandfather. His name was Ernest Herodier. He was a hunter and trapper. The original Herodier was a guide for the RCMP and for surveyors; he delivered mail, he went all along the coast of Hudson Bay, all the way up to Ungava Bay. He was from Fort George. His name was Gaston Herodier, a French guy. Then he had an affair with Hannah Louttit, so they gave their son, Ernest, Gaston's name of Herodier, Snowboy-Herodier.

Then I realized that I could paint and draw so I decided to go to CEGEP [college] with my two girls, which was 1990. I finished the two-year fine arts program. Then I took a year off. Then I went back to the Federal Indian College in Regina, where I got my bachelor of fine arts degree in Indian arts. We come back here to Chisasibi all the time to go in the bush and to see relatives.

What's happened since the hydro project was built scares me. I don't like to see what has happened. There're a lot of good things, like education, the hospital, but I see other things, like what the road has brought in.

The only thing I can do as an artist is to empower people with what their lives are. What they have lived. I'm not outright angry … I'm still angry, though. In writing, too … I find that writing helps.

My kids are going to know both worlds. They are losing their Cree because we have been gone so long. My mother never spoke Cree to us in the house, she spoke only English even though my dad told her to speak Cree to us. I used to wonder why, but now I know why. It just makes me able to communicate better. I didn't speak Cree fluently but I can understand it. I can understand the dialects across Canada. They are very different in Cree.

I feel very Cree. I notice the more I mingle outside, the more Cree I am. It doesn't matter if my dad is Scottish. It's the people who brought me up.

Back here there are not really any job opportunities for me as an artist. I've got to support my family. I might try and get a job in a university or college. I feel like, as an artist, I can do things to help outside the community. People are always happy to see me when I come home. I get a lot of handshakes, hugs, and kisses. Asking, when are you going to come back? Are you going to leave us again? It feels good.

Sometimes I can make a statement with my art, but sometimes I do it just to get it out. Theories—I don't know … sometimes they are visions of just gathering—and I've got to get it out.

"Walk into Life," 1998, step-bite etching by Margaret Orr

Young Community Leaders

At the time that the Quebec government launched the James Bay Project, in 1971, only a small number of young Crees spoke English or had graduated from high school. Only one had gone on to university, and he had dropped out before graduating. To these young people, many of whom were at least partially detached from the traditions of their elders (the very learning of English was enough to achieve that), was given the burden of leading their people in defense of their land, their culture, and their way of life.

Nowadays, the situation is different. Some of the many Crees born since the James Bay and Northern Quebec Agreement was signed are now moving into positions of authority. They have no experience of how their Eeyou Istchee was before the building of the dams and reservoirs. They do not remember the old villages or the days when only a few Crees spoke English or French. They have always lived in a world of TV, VCRs and CDs. Many Crees have graduated from university, many are now studying, and others are on their way to higher education. Though they are interested in the struggles that their parents and grandparents waged, they are uncertain about the best route for their people to follow. These young people sometimes speak of the confusion of living between two cultures, of their own changing attitudes as they become more aware of the Cree values they have inherited, and of the challenges they confront to preserve the Cree way of life while also forging ahead with new ways of being Cree and living in Eeyou Istchee.

Freddy Bosum, 28

University student and local activist

I was born in Chibougamau, where I went to school for a number of years. My mother was working in a sawmill and my dad in a mine. Because my parents went out into the bush and hunted and trapped, I went to different places quite a bit. Most of the time, I was raised by the schools. [My parents] took me into the bush once only because I got kicked out of school. Actually, they took me for a Christmas holiday and I just stayed. It was one of the best years of my life.

I can only hope our Cree life will survive; it would be sad if it is lost. I think one of the worst things you can do to a Native person is you destroy their environment, you take away their independence, you take away their pride. That leads to all kinds of problems.

I was brought up to be in school. My grandparents were in the bush and my brother was living with them. Many times I envied him that lifestyle. Later on, my values got a little confused when I was in school and I didn't know what direction I wanted to go. In those days, I always looked at our people as being very weak. Because my grandparents used to have so much patience, I looked on that as a weakness rather than a strength. Later on, I identified it as a strength. When I was asked to join a negotiation team, I realized how hard it was to get anywhere with the government. And then I came to realize that [the Crees'] patience was a strength rather than a weakness. My values have changed quite a bit over the years.

I went to school in Chapais and lived with my aunt there. I went to school in Mistissini for quite a number of years, right up until my high school years. And then I went to school in Chibougamau. My parents were there at that time. We had grown apart at that point. As most young people would probably say, "My parents don't care about me." That was my philosophy. I figured out later on that they actually cared about me but they just didn't show it in the way that I expected.

Toward the end of high school, secondary four and five, I was not very serious about school in general. But later on I had a life-changing experience. I was supposed to be hopping on a plane up North to one of the Cree communities. I was on this committee which was supposed to establish one of the first Youth Councils. And I saw this older woman and her son trying to get on the plane. The son was on standby and I wasn't. The mother was quite nervous about going back to town, drinking and not showing up for the plane, or whatever. It was the first time that I told myself, "Wait a minute, other people come first, before me."

I think from that point, my whole life direction changed. Rather than try to live for myself, I try to help other people. As soon as I finished high school, I started working at the band office as the first youth coordinator for this community [Oujé-Bougoumou], even though we didn't yet have a community set up. Then I was the chairperson of the Youth Council. I went back to school, although I didn't have a specific focus where I

wanted to be. I took what they call an Explorations Program, which allowed me to study anything. I knew that I wanted to take social science, but before social science I wanted to take some business courses.

After about a year of telling our youth that school is important, I decided to be an example of what I was saying rather than just saying the words, and let my actions do the talking.

I was in Quebec at St. Lawrence College, which was supposed to be a very tough school. I went there for two years. Then I came home for a little while and then I went to Heritage College, in Hull [Quebec]. After that I was getting bored with college so I decided to go to university instead. I took off for Trent University [in Ontario] to take a Native Studies course. A very fascinating school; an odd little town but a very good school with good teachers.

Right now I'm replacing somebody here in the village who has taken a maternity leave. She used to work as manager of the social development programs that we established here in Oujé-Bougoumou to try and create some jobs and business opportunities. Some people have some problems with the Cree language when they try and go to school. So we've created some programs to help them get further in their education. Whether it's in college, university, high school or for specific courses, whether it's truck driving, welding, whatever it is. There's also some recognition awards established under the social development programs—for athletic achievement, academic achievement, and a whole bunch of other awards.

To be a Cree in the modern world means that I come from a people that survive on a land, which some people would describe as harsh and unhabitable. So I come from very strong people. People who have their own set of values, their own language, their own lifestyle—until it was rudely interrupted by what we call the modern society, which seems to be oppressing our people in one way or another.

I look at it as different stages. First they try to take away our identity, try to take our independence—they take away just about everything. Yet we still struggle on, so I think there should be a lot of pride in the fact that we are still here and that we still have our language. I think that's a big, big plus for us.

I struggle like everyone else to try to emulate what the Cree values are supposed to be teaching. To be helpful to anybody that needs help. To share what you have. The only struggle that I have is that I don't mind sharing as long as that person makes an effort. So, basically, I always say that I help those who want to help themselves. I don't share just for the sake of giving. That's the struggle I have with myself.

I like a lot of the Cree values. However, I see a lot of them sort of slipping away, because we are introduced to a system where we are supposed to be paid for everything we do. When we give a piece of meat to an elder we are supposed to be paid for it, that's what I see in the non-Aboriginal system. But I think there are a few people who are living examples of what Cree values should be. I hope someday I will be one of those people.

There are some people like Sam Bosum, the chief; Albert Mianscum is a wonderful teacher, a wonderful speaker; Kenny Mianscum, a number of people in the village. Not a large number of people, mind you, but a number of people nonetheless. There are a few people who still hold something of the traditional values. Still, they are struggling with what I call another stage of the oppression we feel as Native people, which is that we've learned to accept—the housing, the cars that sort of tie you down from the freedom that you used to have as a Native person. You'd take off whenever you wanted, and go hunting and fishing. Now you've got to think, "Oh, wait a minute, I've got to worry about my car payments. I've got to worry about this and that." So you get tied up and a part of you is taken away when you get tied up like that. I think working is a choice that people make. It is part of their responsibility to make those choices but I think in many cases the choices are made for us. I don't know, it's sort of a rough introduction into the modern world.

I'm optimistic as long as we have a few people who still maintain the traditional values. I think that's what holds our people together. I think it's reinforced by the fact that we still maintain our language, we still have certain skills that allow us to survive in the bush, which allow us to have a certain relationship with the land.

I prefer to live here in Oujé-Bougoumou. I would never imagine myself living in a city. Although I may live in a city from time to time, this is always my home. I usually get homesick whenever I'm in a city; after six or eight weeks I get really, really homesick. Homesick for the food, homesick for the air, homesick for the pine trees—just about everything. I come home to recharge again and then I'm ready to go back and face the rest of the world.

Once in a while I go hunting. In the past little while I haven't had too much time. That's not a major part of my attachment right now. I hope that someday I will be able to go out and live the way my people used to live. The way my grandfather used to live. That's still part of my life goals. For me, it's not so much going into the bush once a month as probably two or three times a year for a couple of weeks at a time.

One of the main reasons I went to school was to be able to communicate with non-Native society about the importance of the environment to our people. But I don't think I can effectively communicate that to people just as a translator. I do know the importance of certain things but I haven't had the experience of living in the bush extensively like a lot of our people. That part of it is still missing. I think I would be much more effective if I were able to do that.

Daniel Mark Stewart, 21

Youth representative on the elders' council

I was supposed to start school at the age of four but my grandparents decided I should go out in the bush for one year. We ended up staying two years. Whenever I have the time, I usually go back to the bush. My dad passed away when I was about four years old and ever since then I have lived with my grandparents. From what I hear, my grandfather was one of the great hunters. A couple of years ago, my grandfather passed away from leukemia. I've been living with my grandmother ever since.

I went to school right here in Eastmain, from Grade 1 to secondary five. I graduated about three years ago. I never had to go through a residential school, and I consider myself lucky, from some of the things I heard that students had to go through.

Ever since I graduated, I've been involved with the community. Somebody gave me this idea to maybe stick around for a while and learn from people. Eventually, when I'm ready, I guess I will head back to college and university. I've always wanted to be a lawyer since the first time I saw a movie about lawyers, when I was about seven. I'll probably eventually try to go to law school. I'm thinking about going back to school next fall, depending on the outcome of the elections here. I might run for councillor and if I don't win, I'll head back to school. If I do win, I'll stick around to complete my three-year mandate.

I'd probably go to school in Montreal. I've got a few friends there. I've visited Montreal quite a few times and it looks like a nice place to go to school. I've never lived in a city, except that when I was young, I lived in Montreal with my uncle for about six months during the summer. He was going to school there. I came back in the winter to finish the other half of my school year. That's the only time I've lived down south.

I pretty much learned every skill that I have, everything that I know about hunting and life in general, from my grandparents.

I think I'm capable enough to live down there. I have a general idea of what to expect. I've visited other cities like New York, Atlanta, Florida—I even went to a conference in New Zealand. It was the fifth World Indigenous Youth Conference. I went with the Cree delegation to Waitangi. That's the oldest village in New Zealand, from what I've heard. I really liked it there. We saw a lot of Maoris because they were organizing the conference. In a way I feel fortunate. Like, not everybody in the world has the things that we have here. Yet some people think that we are not fortunate enough. I'm very glad to have the Cree School Board, the Cree Health Board; I'm very grateful. Some people think that's not even enough. From what I've seen of some other Indigenous people, I feel very fortunate.

I was appointed to sit on the local Youth Council, right from when I graduated from high school. And I've been involved in many things at the local level. I've travelled with Chief Gilpin and I've spoken on behalf of the local youth. I was sort of appointed to be the youth spokesperson for a few of the trips that the Chief made to places like Montreal, where we had to meet with the government. I was involved with the negotiations with the Quebec government when we wanted to have this [recreation] building. They wanted elders and youth to be involved.

I've been giving my time for free. How do I live? I guess the way I have made a living has been through travelling. I've been doing that the last few years. The money I get for my meals, I usually save it up and that's how I make a living these days, but it's not easy. I'll probably get my reward at the end. But at the same time, I'm learning, and that's what I'm after.

I've had the privilege of talking to the people who were directly involved with negotiating the James Bay Agreement. Like Ted Moses, Billy Diamond. I think I have a general idea of what's in the Agreement. When I first heard about it, I was in secondary two [Grade 8], I think. That was not too long ago. And ever since I heard about it, I've been talking to people: the people who were involved, like the chiefs who were there. And I've been trying to educate myself on what happened.

Somebody told me that in order to know where you're going, you have to learn from the past, and that's what I've been doing. I've been learning from the James Bay and Northen Quebec Agreement but not only that. I've also been learning about the Cree/Naskapi Act.

What do I think of it? From what I've heard, it was done pretty fast. You can tell it was done pretty fast. A lot of things were missed out and a lot of things could have been done differently. The reason why it's the way it is, I guess, is that at that time we didn't have any Cree lawyers working on it. The first time I read it, I had a hard time understanding what I was reading. You can tell that the Agreement was made up by lawyers. It's not very clear. From what I've heard, there are 350 things that have not been implemented.

They are already talking about another one. But I feel that they have to implement all the things they were supposed to implement, and then I don't see why we have to go along with other future development.

I was asked to sit on the new Cree government board but I decided not to. I was working at that time and I didn't have the time for it. Matthew Mukash made a presentation at the General Assembly this summer about the Cree Nation government, about some of the things that they hope will be changed. I was very much into what they were talking about. I would like to see the Crees be on their own. Self-government, I guess. Maybe even have something that is similar to what the people in Nunavut did. That's the vision I have for the Cree Nation at this time. To be independent and have our own territory.

Here in Eastmain, I sit on the elders' council as a youth representative and I've been learning a lot from them. I've been very curious to hear what they have to say. I'm constantly learning from elders. Like I've been living with elders all my life. I've been constantly learning from them, how to live my life to its fullest. How to enjoy what I have, which is the land and the things that go with it. I've been learning a lot from them and have a lot of respect for elders.

I hunt and fish whenever I have the time. Usually I'm busy but I try and make time. For fishing I usually go out every weekend. But as for hunting, usually it's in the fall and the spring.

This summer I was nominated to be the Cree youth ambassador. As a kid, I used to see the adults drinking and now it's sort of turned around and it's the young people who have started to drink. Drugs as well. Personally, I accept the things that were done in the past and I don't think of us as a colonized people. I don't see it that way. Sure, they made mistakes in the past but we can learn from those mistakes. There are some things that are good to learn from the past but I don't really go out to get the negative things from the past. I want a positive change for the future.

Tony Gull, 22
Economic development officer

Tony Gull of Waswanipi, aged 22 and father of two children, has recently returned to work in a Cree community after spending years pursuing his education in southern, non-Native communities. Though respectful of Cree traditions, he doesn't know how to hunt or trap. Tony respects Cree traditions and clings to his heritage as he dreams of establishing a viable business economy in Wemindji, which has an unemployment rate of 40 percent.

I was born two years after the signing of the James Bay and Northern Quebec Agreement. But I've looked at a lot of the videotapes, the news, the old stuff that happened and I've heard stories from the chiefs who signed the agreements. My grandparents told me about it and a lot of the business people I talk to these days, they learned a lot from what happened back then.

Basically, in my job we provide business assistance to the local entrepreneurs and promote economic development as much as possible in the community. Right now we are kind of focused on mining. We recently set up a company called Wemindji Exploration Incorporated. It's been almost two years now that we've been training those guys in exploration and prospecting. The guys have a lot of dreams; they want to become entrepreneurs, geologists. They like prospecting.

We have four independent businesses here: the taxi, the Wichti Services, which is a painting and plastering business, and then there are two restaurants. When we think

about economic development, we have to make sure that it's feasible for the environment. That's why now we're trying to study the mining industry as much as we can and we're sending our mining guys to different conferences, seminars, and training. All the hunters, trappers, and ouchimaw basically are prospectors. They don't know it but they are, because they bring rocks to us every time they go inland or out on the coast.

As you realize, not many people here are skilled and educated but that's what we need in every community—knowledgeable people. I went to college and I focused mostly on economic development. I'm still taking a university program in economic development at the University of Waterloo. I have to say the traditional Cree values mean a lot to me. I always keep them in mind in what we are doing. But I haven't really acquired any skills of hunting and trapping. So that's one of the things we are going to be setting as one of our priorities: to educate our local youth in our hunting and trapping ways. A lot of our youth in every Cree community don't understand the real skills and knowledge of how to hunt and trap. I'm still in the learning process and I'm 22.

I lived with my grandparents when I was younger and I was brought up to respect my land. Respect all the resources we have. They always mentioned to me that if I attended school and became educated I'd be able to help our people. My grandmother teaches cultural stuff in Waswanipi, all the traditional ways of how to cook. That's one thing I'm never going to let go is my traditional background. My cultural background. I've listened to the elders and I always mention to the young people that you should always listen, that's the only way you'll learn. Listen to everything that people say.

Mostly these days, the elderly people tend to eat the more traditional foods but the younger generation tend to be eating more of the groceries and the produce from the community store. Personally, I tend to mostly rely on the store because I don't hunt yet and because I've just moved into this community. I was always in southern communities going to school, pursuing my education, and I didn't really stay in the Native communities.

This proposed new deal with Hydro-Québec will have a big impact on hunters, trappers, and Cree people in general. But I always think about things not only traditionally, I think about them economically. I think big. I think that within this hydro dam project, we can renegotiate our James Bay and Northern Quebec Agreement. That's the way I feel. It's all I hear about is the James Bay and Northern Quebec Agreement, section this and section that, that haven't been implemented.

We were forced into it. Basically, I find the James Bay Agreement was all planned by the government, even by the lawyers that were working for us, I figure. Because there are certain little things that we know these days that we could have had control over. But now we don't have total control.

Sometimes White outfitters come to our Category 1 and 2 lands, which is not permitted to them under the hunting and trapping laws that were put into the Agreement. Inlanders come into our community or coastal people go inland; that is also

There's a lot of potential in the small community of Wemindji and in every other community. But we need to get educated. We do have a lot of educated people but a lot of them tend to be stuck in terms of funding. I guess you could say that we didn't really use our money properly. That's the way I look at it these days. We haven't really used our resources, we just used them for hunting and trapping.

what's happening. But why are we arguing about that? Why don't we just be together and just hunt and trap wherever we want to, the way it used to be?

I think 20, 30 years ahead, the population will probably double, according to the socio-economic studies we have done for this community. I think our community will probably be as big as Chisasibi. According to my analysis, our unemployment rate here is practically 40 percent. We have ten businesses: three independent and seven under our government. We have several entrepreneurs who want to set up their own businesses. One entrepreneur is starting a tourism project. He's going to build some sort of lodge, with parking spaces, a beach, a walking area. We plan to implement a little tourist attraction of our peninsula and our bay out there, where you'll be able to take pictures and have a nice nature walk.

A lot of the hunters, trappers, and people are not too happy. Ever since I was a young boy, that's all I've heard talk about, just bands and banks and Hydro-Québec and it's like they are the enemy; more, I guess, from a business perspective—it was a good joint venture but it wasn't set up right the first time; it didn't turn out good for us. It was just like a short-term thing and that was it. But now we have our negotiators out there and they know how to deal with these issues. We still have the consultants that are helping us; hopefully, the big men up there will make the right decisions.

Creating Cree Community

Throughout their history, the James Bay Crees have travelled from their far-flung hunting camps to come together at summer fishing sites, or in historic times, trading posts. Creating community is as much a tradition of the Cree way of life as hunting, trapping, and fishing have been. In the last century, the invasive influence of outside forces has had a drastic effect on their traditional practices of community building. Yet, the continual efforts and energies of the Crees to gather their resources and support their communities, despite the obstacles and inaction of governments, have been unfailing.

When the Crees signed the 1975 James Bay and Northern Quebec Agreement, they did so with the understanding that the hydroelectric energy development projects in Eeyou Istchee were intended to be sources of employment, business development, and contract opportunities for the Crees throughout their traditional territory. Not only was it expected that these economic activities would contribute to positive social and community development in Eeyou Istchee, but specific government responsibilities for ensuring economic and social development were also addressed in the Agreement. However, it was not long after the signing that the Crees realized that the governments of Canada and Quebec had no real plans regarding when and how to implement the development that had been promised in such areas as health and social services, education, policing, administering justice, local and regional government, and economic and social development.

While the hydroelectric development went ahead, government action to meet their treaty obligations did not. In some cases, the Crees used their own compensation funds to begin community initiatives, and sued the governments afterwards for repayment and damages. It took serious incidents such as gastroenteritis outbreaks, terrible housing conditions, and court actions to draw attention to the governments' negligence in their obligations to provide basic community services. Even then, this situation at first got real attention only when the Crees exposed such negligence to the parliamentary Standing Committee on Aboriginal Affairs.

In the years since the signing of the 1975 treaty, the Crees have pursued the rights that they were guaranteed under it and, mostly through their own efforts, considerable progress has been made in the social development of their communities. The treaty provided for Cree control of health and school boards and, while the governments ignored or argued about their obligations in these areas, the Crees pressed on and used these institutions to address educational and health needs of the Eeyouch. Sometimes the only route was to take court actions, sometimes they ran deficits to address crucial needs and always they kept their efforts in the public eye.

In all the work they had to do, they did not forget about their lost community, the displaced Eeyouch of Oujé-Bougoumou. Dispersed due to mining development on their traditional lands, the Oujé-Bougoumou Crees were without a community to call their own. As a result, they ceased to exist on official records and were even excluded from the discussions leading up to the 1975 Agreement. Nonetheless, with the help of the Grand Council of the Crees, the people of Oujé-Bougoumou did eventually secure land and build their own community, a modern-traditional village in Eeyou Istchee.

The following stories of the Cree School Board, the Cree Board of Health and Social Services, and the community of Oujé-Bougoumou reveal an important part of the Crees' commitment and insistance to determine their own destiny as a People.

The Cree School Board: A Vehicle for Community and Cree Nation Development

The link between the past and the future is perhaps nowhere more relevant than in the area of Cree education.

Paul Gull, Chairman of the Cree School Board, 1993

Cree education was a cornerstone of the 1975 James Bay and Northern Quebec Agreement. Section 16 of the Agreement established a new body, the Cree School Board, to take responsibility for educating Cree youths and adults and preparing them to deal with the modernization that the proposed development of the James Bay area would bring. The Agreement gave the new school board special powers to design, in conjunction with the Quebec Department of Education and the Government of Canada, an education system that could be specifically oriented to Cree needs. With this step, the Crees seized control of their education and gained the ability to protect their language and culture. The Crees could decide the language of instruction, choose the curriculums, select appropriate textbooks, hire appropriate teachers (Aboriginal and non-Aboriginal), and adopt a distinctly Cree school calendar.

John Blueboy, Inventor of the Decorative Decoy

The 1975 Agreement outlined the composition of the Cree School Board: it was to include school commissioners elected from each Cree community, and committees for each elementary and high school. Committee composition was to include band council and parent representatives, thus ensuring community involvement in educational decision-making.

The Cree School Board was formally constituted under the Quebec Education Act in 1978, and 1978-79 was the first official school year under the new Board. The early years were difficult. The Board inherited three school systems (federal, provincial, and missionary), which it had to integrate into one. The Board members were not daunted, however, and took up the challenge of developing a uniquely Cree education system that would enable young and old (through continuing education programs) to follow a traditional way of life and still participate in the modern world.

A New Kind of Education for the Crees

In Cree culture, receiving an education has always meant being taught the Cree way of life in the bush. A person is taught the traditions, including the details of how to survive on the land and the stories, legends, and prophecies that are handed down from generation to generation. This knowledge is imparted gradually as a person grows up and is capable of understanding and using the knowledge.

European-style schooling for the Crees was first introduced in the 19th century. It came as day schools in the summer months, when the people came together around the trading posts. English missionaries brought this type of schooling with them and developed a system of syllabics so the Crees could write in their own language and translate the gospel and religious songs. James Evans, the Methodist missionary who invented the Cree syllabary, believed that the Crees must be able to read and write in their own language if they were to benefit from Christian teachings. He developed the Cree syllabary as a phonetically based system because it was thought to be more representative of the Cree language than standard roman lettering.

The Crees accepted the summer schools, seeing this first schooling as an opportunity to learn more about European ways. The schools provided an opportunity for some of their children to learn English (and later French, when the James Bay territories were ceded to the Province of Quebec in 1898). They saw the advantages of breaking away from the often overbearing control that the Hudson's Bay Company exerted over their lives, largely because its employees and managers could speak English and therefore acted as arbiters of the relations between the Eeyouch and the rest of the non-Aboriginal world. However, schooling was also something that was introduced from outside Cree culture. It was something over which Cree parents had no control, other than allowing their children to attend classes.

Taking Control of the Education System

The Euro-Canadian philosophy of the 19th century was that the Aboriginal way of life was somehow primitive and that Aboriginal people needed to be given moral and religious direction. By the early 20th century, separating Aboriginal children from their families and sending them away from their communities to residential schools (described on page 23) was seen as the best strategy to educate Aboriginal children. The Anglican Church, and later the Roman Catholic Church, were put in charge of setting up these schools in the James Bay territory. The first school was in Moose Factory, Ontario. Later, two residential schools were built in what was known as Fort George (now Chisasibi), Quebec.

In the beginning, the use of the Cree language, Eeyiyouayiminanouch, was tolerated in the schools as was the teaching of syllabics. However, eventually the use of Eeyiyouayiminanouch was discouraged and then forbidden. Moreover, even though the

Invention of the Cree Syllabary

James Evans was born in Hull, England in 1801, and emigrated to Canada in 1823. He was given responsibility for the Methodist mission school at Rice Lake in Upper Canada, in 1828. In 1836, he completed a syllabic version of the Ojibway language and submitted it to the Bible Society in Toronto, but it was rejected. In 1837, he published *The Speller and Interpreter*, in Indian and English, a grammar of the Ojibway language that included hymns and portions of the scriptures translated into Ojibway. Three years later, the Wesleyan Missionary Society in England appointed him Superintendent of Missions in the Hudson Bay territory.

There he invented, in 1840, the Cree syllabic alphabet, based on his earlier syllabary of the Ojibway language. The original version of the syllabary employed about 49 characters, which created a written language that could be adapted for all branches of the Algonquian language and for other Native languages as well.

The earliest known printed example of the Cree syllabic script is reproduced on the front cover of James Evans' *Cree Syllabic Hymn Book*. It is the earliest book extant that is known to have been printed in the Canadian Northwest. Printed on a converted fur press (a press used to tightly pack furs for shipping) at Norway House, Hudson Bay territory, the type used had been cast from lead obtained partly from the lining of tea chests and partly from bullets. Only three copies of the book are known to be in existence.

Eventually, the Cree syllabary moved its way through all the Algonquian tribes. The Anglican Church adapted it for the Moose Factory Cree (Ontario) in 1851 and, in 1871, the Catholic Church adopted it for use in the Catholic missions.

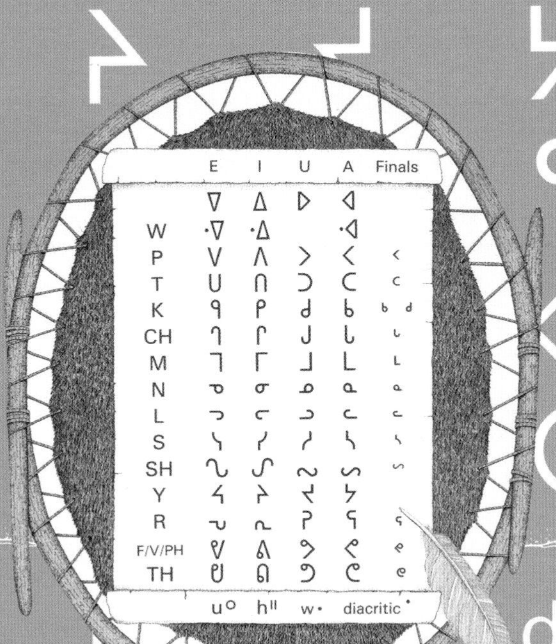

schools were in Cree communities, communication between the students and the community was restricted.

The non-Native agenda was to assimilate Eeyou children into the non-Native society. However, many parents kept some of their children away from school so that they could grow up on the land and live as their fathers and mothers had before them, as owners of their family hunting lands. As they continued to trade furs and to derive a way of life from the land, the Cree way of life seemed secure.

In the 1960s, the churches lost control of the schools to the governments of Canada and Quebec. Aboriginal leaders began to criticize the whole system of schooling, from its assimilationist curriculum and organization to the lack of involvement of Aboriginal peoples in determining its direction. By the late 1960s and early 1970s, the first Eeyouch graduated from the school system and were jolted into action by the announcement of the first phase of the James Bay hydroelectric development project. With the Cree way of life and lands threatened by proposed flooding, young graduates joined Cree leaders and began their work to force the larger society to take note of the Eeyouch and their rights.

In retrospect, there is irony in the fact that the first crop of graduates from this repressive and assimilationist education system were the ones to champion Cree rights. Even with all of its flaws, the school system was teaching many very resourceful Eeyouch how to interact with the world outside Eeyou Istchee. They were the first to realize that the system that had been set up to assimilate them could be used to help them fight back.

Earlier in this book, Ted Moses recalls the Crees' efforts to stop the hydroelectric projects. As court actions and negotiations concerning the hydroelectric projects were initiated between the Crees and opposing governments and corporations, young English-speaking Crees were called upon to act as translators for their chiefs and elders.

Poor Conditions in Schools

At the time of the 1975 Agreement, the schools were foreign territory to the parents. Most communities had day schools, but these were foreign implants in the communities. Some teachers tried to bring elements of Cree culture into the classroom, but there was no formal institutional support for such efforts. An assimilationist strategy was alive and well in those schools, even though they provided primary education in the communities. The teachers lived, for the most part, in what was referred to as "Federal Square," an enclave of townhouses where their social life went on oblivious to the surrounding community. Of course, there were individual exceptions to this, but the majority of the teachers had problems dealing with Cree culture and the lack of facilities and services. The stress of doing this both in and outside the classroom was daunting to them.

In most communities, there were no parent committees to guide the operation of the schools. Cree was not accepted as the language of instruction, so the children went from homes where they spoke nothing but Cree, to schoolrooms where English (and in some schools French) was the only language used. Moreover, because the communities were isolated and almost all parents lived from hunting, it was not particularly evident to the children what relevance much of what they were being taught would have in their lives.

The schools were also in poor condition. They were cold and did not meet provincial or federal standards. They were to some degree dangerous, as the heating systems were often inadequate and poorly designed and maintained. For example, the boiler in St. Philip's School in Fort George (Chisasibi) often broke down and was in danger of exploding. All of the schools were in need of replacement by larger and safer buildings.

Grand Chief Ted Moses

This in itself was an education for these young graduates, and their roles eventually evolved beyond mere translation to political activism and involvement. These political battles also provided them with an opportunity to address very high level representatives of the governments of Canada and Quebec.

The Crees demanded changes to repressive government policies that sought to "integrate" Aboriginal people at the expense of their culture and language. Although many Crees felt that the James Bay and Northern Quebec Agreement that was eventually signed in 1975 did not go far enough in securing Cree rights, the Agreement was, in many respects, ahead of its time. The fact remains that the 1975 Agreement set up the only Aboriginal school board, and health and social services board, in Canada.

Strengthening the Community Schools

When Cree representatives were negotiating for their own school board, they realized that the schools in the communities had been underfunded up to that point and had been cared for poorly. There were many reasons for this: the communities thought of the schools as belonging to the Canadian government, parents were not involved with the schools, and the teachers were responsible to administrators from outside the Cree culture. For these administrators, keeping expenses down was the "name of the game."

The community schools were unhappy places, and there was a high rate of teacher turnover. When the school year ended, there was often only the local janitor around to care for the place. Nobody was there to think about ordering the supplies for the next year. As a result, when the new term began, the new teachers would not have supplies.

Knowing this, Cree leaders negotiated for a local education administrator for each community. The administrator would be a local person and would work with the teachers and principal to ensure that curriculum materials and supplies would be ordered. This person would also act as a local advocate for the decisions of the school committees, which were to be set up under the Cree School Board.

For the first 10 years, the Board turned its attention to building new schools and the offices it needed in order to operate. All of the schools from the previous system had to be replaced because they were too small and they were in poor condition. Also, since the Board's inception, three communities have been moved or created anew (the community of Fort George was moved to accommodate the huge dam that was built at the mouth of the La Grande River, and the community was recreated as Chisasibi) and have required new schools.

In the early days of planning, the school board struggled with cost and infrastructure issues. The board members considered such options as having one high school service

Artist: Edna Blueboy, 12 years old, Wiinibekuu School

We had to train the teachers, give them a 10-course, 30-credit certificate program in Aboriginal literacy. The first group of 48 teachers completed the course in 1999. A second group started in 2000. It takes two or three years. The staff here designed the courses, with McGill University. The courses are held in the communities, and some at the university.

Those specially trained teachers are already working in the school system. When we asked them to teach in Cree, some who were already teaching in the second languages—English or French—were very reluctant. In a way we had to sort of force them. We told them it had been decided. Some of them didn't feel confident to read and write the language, although they spoke Cree. Now they are good. They are enthusiastic, but we still encounter some problems and need to improve a lot.

Daisy Herodier
Teacher and Coordinator of the Cree Language Programme
Cree School Board

several communities. But it was soon recognized that the days of residential schools—and of boarding arrangements that centralized the students in one community—were over. Parents demanded that their children attend school in their home communities. Today, each Cree community runs its own school under the overall management of the Cree School Board, working with the Quebec Department of Education.

Celebrating the Achievements

When the Eeyouch took control of the education of their children, Eeyiyouayiminanouch was brought back into the schools and it was taught by Eeyou teachers. For this to happen, the Board had to set up a system of teacher training and a whole department of curriculum development.

Today, students are taught in their own language for the first three years of school. After that, Eeyiyouayiminanouch is taught as a subject in all years. The English and French languages are introduced only once the students are fluent in their own language and have grasped the syllabic writing system. Incentives are given to students to excel in studies of their own culture and language. Eeyouch-developed curriculum materials are provided, in English and French, that give a more accurate description of history than the often patronizing and false representation of Aboriginal peoples found in materials used in most Canadian schools.

The Cree School Board has implemented a distance education program, where the latest in video broadcast technology is used to increase the variety and number of course opportunities open to secondary and post-secondary students in the communities. Also, the majority of the teachers in the schools, the administrators of the schools, and the members of the Board are Crees.

In the past 25 years, hydroelectric development projects and forestry activities have knocked Cree families off traditional family hunting lands. The traditional way of Cree life, based on harvesting animals and using the resources of the whole territory to benefit communities, fit very well with the fur trade and was, to some degree, exploited by that trade. However, the fur trade is no longer an economically viable way of life. A beaver pelt that sold for $40 in 1940 still sells today for $40, but the cost of living is much higher.

These factors, and the progressive diversification and centralization of work opportunities in the communities, mean that many Cree children today have little opportunity to experience life on the land. Since the Agreement was signed in 1975 approximately one-third of Cree families now derive their primary source of income from working for local band administrations. The Cree School Board, Health Board, other regional Cree entities, local companies, and other businesses employ many Crees. As well, approximately one-third between the ages of 18 and 65 are involved in full-time hunting, fishing, and trapping. Nonetheless, there is a 28 percent unemployment rate among Cree people in James Bay. Each year approximately 250 people are added to the labour force as they reach working age.

With established communities and such diverse employment opportunities, many children do not learn the traditions and the skills of living from the land, traditions that many in the previous generation also missed because of attendance at residential schools. To compensate for this, the Board has implemented a program to take the students out to traditional bush camps where they can learn traditional Cree skills. In these times of rapid economic and social change, a firm understanding of life on the land and knowledge of the Cree language help students to develop a strong sense of identity and self-confidence while growing up.

But teaching Cree traditions is not the only priority. The Board has improved the academic achievement of the Eeyouch. Today, over 400 Cree students are pursuing post-secondary education. Among them are students of medicine, engineering, and teaching, as well as many of the trades so needed in the communities.

Looking to the Future

The greatest challenge facing the Cree School Board today is to improve the quality of the academic education received by the students and to maintain and improve the Cree content of the curriculum. In part, this effort will depend on the economic opportunities open to Cree students once they graduate. Students coming through the education system must have experience and knowledge of the many careers from which they can choose. In the coming years, the Board plans to put greater emphasis on adult education and courses to help Crees in their career development.

The Board has recognized that increasing the emphasis on career development must coincide with increasing liaison efforts with the companies that are active in the Cree territory. In Eeyou Istchee, 14,000 people derive their incomes directly or indirectly from the forestry industry. Of these, only 50 or so are Crees, and they are working in the industry only because the Crees themselves invested millions of dollars in a sawmill. Of the over 600 people working directly and indirectly for Hydro-Québec on the long-term maintenance of the La Grande Project, six Crees have jobs. The spinoff jobs in hydroelectricity, forestry, and mining activities on the territory—and a vast majority of the salaries paid—go directly to non-Crees and non-Cree companies.

The Cree School Board aims to liaise with industries for the purpose of developing career counselling programs, summer employment programs, and employment information initiatives for students at all levels. Representatives from these companies will be invited to be more present in Cree schools, to show students what is available, and to help develop the career training and academic education paths that are necessary to provide students with access to all types of jobs.

The Board now provides services to over 3,500 students at the elementary, secondary, and post-secondary levels. Current programs, which focus on the needs of the communities, are being strengthened on an ongoing basis. Crees and the Cree School Board are also looking outside their communities to activities and development occurring throughout the whole of Eeyou Istchee. In keeping with the spirit that helped create the Cree School Board, Crees continue to see the Board as an instrument to break down racial barriers and to bring Cree and non-Cree people together to work in industry.

Artist: Darren Moar, 12 years old, Wiinibekuu School

Living Well and Healing on Eeyou Istchee

The Cree Medicine Chest

Eeyou traditional medical practices have probably changed little since the start of the last millennium. As with all aspects of Eeyou life, the environment provided the ingredients needed to make natural medicines. The Eeyou medicine chest contained animal, plant, and mineral elements, which were collected for future medicinal use as the Eeyouch came across them in their travels.

Labrador tea provided large doses of vitamin C, which cured loose teeth and bleeding gums, and prevented colds or hastened their end. Charcoal, obtained by burning certain woods, was used to combat diarrhea. Tamarack and spruce gums were used as antiseptics. They were also used as wound closures for minor cuts and as an adhesive to hold in place bandages made of hide. Even before the arrival of the Europeans, the Eeyouch knew about the importance of cleaning wounds carefully, applying antiseptics, preparing clean dressings, and cauterizing severe wounds with a hot object.

Fish broth was given for indigestion. Infusions of beaver musk (castoreum) and Labrador tea were used to treat urinary infections. Impetigo and scabies were treated with creeping snowberry, cattails, and cow parsnip. Boils and abscesses were treated with hot or cold compresses made with ash, birch, and tamarack. Sore throats were treated with a tincture made by boiling alder or cattails. While there were remedies for mild pain, severe and chronic pain were usually managed through the application of heat (using hide-wrapped hot rocks or sand), massage, and spiritual discipline.

Generally, people kept some medicines for immediate use and collected others as the need and opportunity arose. There was also some trade of medicinal ingredients among the different communities. Nothing of value was overlooked.

Warm blankets, birchbark buckets of steaming water, pulverized cedar bark plasters, and the sweat lodge were used to fight colds or other infections. The Eeyouch had no idea that their bodies were fighting an invasion of invisible creatures called bacteria or viruses. They also did not know that these survive only in a very narrow range of body temperature. What they did know was that warmth speeds healing. It did not matter to them that they were elevating blood temperature to help the white corpuscles of the body's immune system. All that mattered was that what they did worked and always had worked.

But traditional medical practices of the Eeyouch encompassed more than just the knowledge of how to use medicines. The approach to health and healing was a holistic one—understood by all members of the community—that relied on traditional concepts of social relations, knowledge of the environment, and ideas about healing and its spiritual aspects.

The Eeyouch have always been a tough and resourceful people. They did not have the luxury of reporting in sick when they had a cold, a headache, or a cut thumb. Their environment was bountiful, but it could also be unforgiving. Every Eeyou had at least an elementary knowledge of "bush medicine." The lone hunter with a cut and twisted ankle

The Eeyouch lived in small groups where everyone had a productive role. All community members were keenly aware that the loss of one person's contribution, even for a short while, was felt by all and in some circumstances could be crucial to the survival of the group. Individuals did their utmost to carry on.

often had no choice but to apply a dressing and march back to his group's encampment. As they were dependent on their feet, people were careful to treat any foot infections or injuries before they became disabling.

The sweat lodge was a vital part of the healing cycle. It offered both tangible and intangible benefits. Those who had overexerted themselves used sweats to relax aching muscles. Sweating was also a means of cleansing that was used in the absence of manufactured soap. There was more to sweating than sitting in a hot lodge. It could be used as a time to relax and relieve stress, or else to reflect. It could be a social activity. It could also be part of a healing therapy, under the guidance of a healer.

The Eeyouch were adept at making sweat lodges to accommodate one or more people. Indeed, a lone hunter would not hesitate to build a one-person mitonsanagamuk, or hide-covered dome shaped tent, to use for a sweat. Suitable rocks of certain mineral types were the best at retaining heat and not shattering when water was applied. People took dry sweats or steam sweats, as required.

The Importance of Healers and Community Support

While everyone had a sound working knowledge of bush medicine, those people who were particularly gifted came to be recognized as healers. A healer's skills and knowledge were essential to a community. Certain healing techniques were risky and the average Eeyou would normally not attempt them, for instance setting broken bones or treating hypertension by bloodletting. Healers, often elder women, took exceptional note of the healing knowledge passed down by their elders. In this way, elders who might be incapacitated to some degree still continued to contribute to the group through their knowledge of healing.

Most illnesses were attributed to becoming cold, overheated, or run down by exhaustion or lack of fresh food. Of course, these events could lead to physical and emotional distress, or they could lead to accidents. The Eeyouch also believed that some people, called "mideo" in some dialects, had a special (supernatural) ability to do harm to others. Healers could understand this and deal with these misfortunes.

Healers were often able to cement rifts in the social fabric of the community. They could help the afflicted to confront, understand, and deal with the source of personal grief. They could also mobilize the community to help in the individual's healing, as care was seen to be a community responsibility.

Healers had a special ability to blend the use of medicines that would heal the body physically with a sensitive appreciation of human emotional and spiritual needs. Healers are best described as those who knew what could be done, often in difficult situations, to promote healing. They were very good at observing life around them; they were exceptional listeners and, as a result, their words were very strong.

When someone lost a loved one, the Eeyouch did not have psycho-chemicals to treat depression, but they had each other to draw strength from and receive help from. They also had their faith in the Creator and the interconnectedness of all things. Their beliefs in the traditional laws of nature, and the importance they placed on spiritual and physical balance, gave them a moral code from which they drew strength. And their healers helped fashion these strengths into a healing journey.

The Eeyouch recognized that the health of a community depended on more than the physical and emotional health of its individual members. They had what we think of today as "social services," although many of today's social problems were unthinkable in the past. For example, teen pregnancy was not an issue. Often, people did not get married until they were able to care for a family. For many, this meant living with their parents until they were into their twenties. Sometimes people married at a younger age, but the young couple lived with one of their families (often the bride's family) and worked to contribute to the family's livelihood on the land. Compatibility with in-laws was crucial and, as a result, marriages were often arranged by the parents of the young couples. This did not always produce congenial relationships, but people learned to live and work together in support of the family. Unlike the practice today, new couples did not seek to "move out on their own." They knew that their well-being demanded a household with elders and often other immediate kin. Each had an economic contribution to make.

As with any culture where each individual plays an important role in the survival of the group, there was an agreeable but strict division of responsibilities according to gender, age, and also ability. Today, some of these gender relationships might be called patriarchal or oppressive, but Eeyou society had clear role models for "good husband," "good wife," and even "good bachelor." The Eeyouch of the past were crystal clear about these roles and their accompanying social conventions and, as a result, were highly practical in their social relations.

In the past, households would grow as a result of births and also attachments. For example, orphaned children were usually taken into the next of kin's household, although another family would oblige if it were in a better economic position to provide care. People unable to care for themselves were cared for by the community as a whole. As people

aged and became less self-reliant, their role changed to one of teaching, tutoring, and caring for youth. Their own needs were increasingly provided for as their physical capacities diminished. There were also stern laws against abuse and neglect—elder and child abuse were particularly reviled.

New Threats to Cree Health

In pre-European contact times, Eeyou medicine was adequate for treating the known illnesses and injuries. Undoubtedly, there were fewer serious infectious diseases in the pre-contact era, as the incidence of outsiders coming into the community was much lower. With European contact, new diseases were introduced against which the Eeyouch had little immunity or knowledge of effective treatments. In some parts of the Americas, diseases such as influenza, measles, typhoid, and tuberculosis devastated Aboriginal populations. No doubt there were serious impacts on the health of the Eeyouch, but they were, to some degree, protected from the uncontrolled passage of diseases because they lived in separated family groups.

There were usually two outbreaks of disease per year: in January, when people were more confined within shelters and perhaps weakened by their winter diet; and in late summer, after the ships had come in to restock the trading posts and missions. Understandably, people tried to stay in the bush during the summer epidemic season.

Sometimes the European immigrants who came to Eeyou Istchee to help the inhabitants were part of the problem. For example, the missionaries who arrived in Fort George (now Chisasibi) in the 1800s were also disease carriers. It has been documented that a century ago about 100 Eeyouch died of measles in Fort George alone.

Over the four centuries since European contact, many Eeyouch perished in the bush with no written record. The trading post managers or the missionaries sometimes took note. In later times, the Indian Agent (a representative of the federal Department of Indian Affairs) would provide some minimal funding to reimburse the traders or churches for medicines provided.

In the early 1900s, an influx of independent trappers and hunters caused a collapse in the Eeyou system of land management and this led to famine. In the 1920s, the federal government provided rations to sick and destitute Eeyouch. It also paid for rations issued by the churches, traders, and the Royal Canadian Mounted Police (RCMP).

The Department of Indian Affairs always argued over the cost of rations. In fact, as an economy measure during the Depression, the ration scales were slashed in the early 1930s, when the Eeyouch were in greatest need. Around the same time, measures were instituted by the Eeyouch—in co-operation with the Province of Quebec, the Government of Canada, and the Hudson's Bay Company—to keep the independent trappers and hunters from harvesting in the territory and to reinstate the Cree system of land management based on conservation. While this led to improved incomes and diets, the benefits of this program (e.g. increase in animal populations and Eeyou health) took until the 1940s to come about.

The Transition to Western Medicine

In spite of efforts to improve Eeyou incomes and diets, smallpox, tuberculosis, and pneumonia were prevalent (particularly in the residential schools) in the 1940s and 1950s. Consequently, plans were approved in the early 1940s for the establishment of the first federal nursing station in Eeyou lands, at Fort George (Chisasibi). More were to follow in other locations throughout the territory. Whereas in the past, the churches and trading posts had been the providers of Western medicines, the nursing stations gradually took over this role. Resident nurses did what they could, but were often unable to provide adequate medical assistance. Doctors visited the territory, but their visits were short and infrequent and had little influence in the overall health care provided to the Eeyouch. The Western medicine chest was still limited and its effectiveness against many diseases was questionable. The Eeyouch knew this.

A turning point in Eeyou health came in 1945, when a federal government benefit helped provide foodstuffs (through rations). The federal government's Family Allowance was made available to all families with children. This was Canada's first universal welfare program, meaning that benefits were awarded solely on the basis of age and residence or citizenship, without assessment of the recipient's income or assets. The allowance was provided monthly to families to help cover the cost of raising children.

When the allowance was first introduced, its critics suggested that the money be distributed by way of services rather than by cheque. Supporters of the allowance lobbied against this as the sole approach, arguing that providing the benefit in cash would enhance the autonomy of families. Ironically, not all recipients (for example, the Eeyouch) were to be given the benefit of autonomy.

It seems that Aboriginal people were not trusted with cash, because the Department of Indian Affairs issued their Family Allowance as rations. Many Eeyouch remember the tins of tomato juice and condensed milk, and the identical yellow rubber boots for their children. But even then, there was a catch: Eeyou families would not receive the rations unless they sent their children to the residential schools.

Shortly after the creation of the federal Department of National Health and Welfare in 1944, Indian Health Services was moved from the Department of Indian Affairs to this new department. As a result, Indian health was taken more seriously: more doctors were flown in to Eeyou Istchee for more visits, although just in the summer months at first. Medical teams started inoculating children against diseases and fewer people developed the "killer" diseases. Later, teams came with X-ray machines, and dozens of Eeyouch were diagnosed with tuberculosis. Most were sent to Moose Factory Indian Hospital (built in 1949 and now named the Weeneebayko General Hospital) or to hospitals in the south; some never returned.

The first antibiotic, penicillin, was developed during World War II. For the first time, Western medicine could offer a real cure for many of the terrible infectious diseases, and the Eeyouch began to have more regard for Western medicine. They saw that it could cure the new diseases, against which traditional medicine was powerless. In fact, the Eeyouch had always been fairly open-minded towards new medicines, if there was evidence that they worked. They were not afraid to adopt new ingredients into the traditional medicine chest.

Despite better medical services than in the past, the epidemics were not over. In the early 1950s, influenza killed about 200 people along the coast. There was usually one mild gastroenteritis epidemic each summer. This new threat appeared once people started living in confined areas without proper sanitation facilities. More antibiotics became available, and dentists began visiting the territory by plane. (However, for many years the dentists attended only to Eeyou schoolchildren and the White population.) Gradually, the lifespan of the average Eeyou increased, and the infant mortality rate improved but was still a source of great concern. The population began to edge upwards.

By the 1950s, the federal government had decided that the Eeyou traditional way of life was dying fast and encouraged the Eeyouch (with rations and building materials) to build permanent houses. Unfortunately, water and sewage systems did not follow the building materials. To encourage the establishment of permanent communities, the Eeyouch were also promised jobs, but these did not materialize. In place of jobs, they had welfare.

As was discussed briefly in the article entitled "Quebec Secession and Cree Rights," in the 1960s the Province of Quebec began to pay more attention to the provincial economy and health and education services. Until that time, it had left administration and services in the James Bay region to the federal government. After studying the development potential of Eeyou Istchee, and seeing the potential for developing hydroelectric projects, Quebec now raced to build an administrative presence in the region and to assert its own jurisdiction. Provincial government buildings started appearing in the early 1970s, including the Chisasibi Hospital Centre. It was not built purely for the benefit of the Eeyouch, but also as a central facility for the expected influx of White workers. At first, Quebec would provide services to Aboriginal people only if Canada paid, which it would not. The hospital therefore redirected Eeyouch to the federal clinic in Chisasibi. Most Eeyouch needing hospital services continued to be sent to the Moose Factory Indian Hospital in Ontario.

A New Era for Cree Health and Social Services

Despite the confusion between the federal and provincial roles in the community, and the enduring preference of many Eeyouch for the federal nursing station, the Chisasibi Hospital Centre was administered by a board that included Chisasibi band members. This was the first formal recognition by governments of the importance of involving the Eeyouch in the management of their health facilities.

In 1971, the Eeyouch began their battle against provincial plans to establish hydroelectric megaprojects without Eeyou consent. The resulting treaty, the 1975 James Bay and Northern Quebec Agreement, achieved—among other things—a transfer of federal and provincial infrastructure to Eeyou control. It also recognized the inherent right of the Eeyouch to manage their affairs according to standards appropriate to the needs of the communities. Section 14 of the Agreement provided for Eeyou control of the five federal health stations (at Chisasibi, Waskaganish, Waswanipi, Whapmagoostui, and Mistissini) and the Chisasibi Hospital Centre, under the guidance of the Cree Board of Health and Social Services of James Bay.

The new Cree Board was officially in place by 1978. From the beginning, it faced many of the same problems that other newly created entities faced, and the refusal of the federal and provincial governments to implement their obligations under the Agreement made every attempt to move forward an uphill battle. The Board was to exercise its powers and carry out its functions within the meaning of the Quebec provincial act governing health and social services. With a separatist government in power, however, Quebec refused to accept any responsibility for the federal health clinics unless the Canadian government paid for all operational costs for the first five years! The federal government, which wanted to be rid of the facilities as soon as possible, stopped all regular maintenance and planned upgrades to clinic facilities and programming. The transfer of all five clinics was not completed until 1981; by this time the Board inherited five very rundown facilities along with a grossly inadequate operations budget.

The new Board faced a serious and worsening health and social situation. Its requests for reasonable funding to bring services up to provincial standards were ignored.

The health clinics were small and ill-equipped, and there were no services for counselling those with social or psychological problems. Aside from those working in the provincial hospital in Fort George [Chisasibi], there were no doctors or dentists in the communities. The nurses who worked in the clinics were vastly overworked. They performed emergency procedures that they were not trained to do, because they had to be done.

Liaison with the southern hospitals was primitive. People would be flown south for surgery or some other treatment and little or nothing would be heard about them for weeks or, in some cases, months. Then one day they would show up on the plane, or a message would be received that an anonymous body bag was being shipped up. In some instances, the parents or spouse would be called to come and identify the corpse.

Grand Chief Ted Moses

The withdrawal of federal involvement resulted in the loss of regional-level support functions (e.g. environmental health, public health, a mercury poisoning prevention program, and non-insured benefits administration). Quebec did not fill these gaps in health services, nor did it recognize that the Board should do so. Consequently, serious service gaps developed.

Mercury—A Devastating Side Effect of Development

In 1980, many Eeyouch were exhibiting symptoms of mercury poisoning. The cause of the contamination was a food source—fish from the newly created reservoirs of the hydroelectric development. The decomposition of trees (as a result of the flooding) had created high levels of mercury. Mercury poisoning, and treatment, quickly became an extremely sensitive issue that highlighted deficiencies in Cree medical services. The Cree Board of Health and Social Services of James Bay began its own mercury program in 1982, but the Province of Quebec was very reluctant to provide any funding. It preferred to support the inadequate mercury program of the Montreal General Hospital's Community Health Department. (In fact, after 25 years, the Montreal General continues to deliver public health programs to Eeyouch who are over 1,000 kilometres away.)

Proper funding for a mercury poisoning prevention program was not acquired until the Mercury Agreement was signed with Hydro-Québec and the Province of Quebec in late 1986. The Cree Board was made responsible for the health and social services component. It is fair to say that early interventions, including strong efforts by the Board, have changed Eeyou eating patterns enough to avoid an epidemic of mercury poisonings. However, in 2000 there were still serious concerns that dissuading people from eating fish, to avoid mercury poisonings, was leading to extremely high rates of diabetes among the Eeyouch.

During the summer of 1980, over 80 Eeyouch were hospitalized due to a gastro-enteritis epidemic resulting from a lack of clean water and proper sanitation facilities in the communities, even though these had been promised in the 1975 Agreement. Then in 1981 a tuberculosis epidemic occurred in Mistassini, but Quebec tried to downplay the matter. At this point, the Grand Council of the Crees demanded a federal–provincial inquiry. This was refused. The Quebec provincial government failed to take necessary corrective action, and the Canadian government refused to guarantee Cree health.

Finally, in 1981, the Grand Council was successful in forcing an extensive federal review to be undertaken of the implementation of the James Bay and Northern Quebec Agreement. The review results were published in 1982, and they condemned the federal government for failing to implement commitments in socio-sanitary infrastructure, thereby contributing to the Crees' health problems. The Government of Canada responded to the review with a five-year, $61 million package to improve Cree and Inuit schools, housing, and sanitary facilities like sewers and drinking water. This was a start, although the amount was not based on an assessment of actual needs.

In the same year, the Constitution Act, 1982 was proclaimed. Section 35 of the Constitution protected "existing" treaty and Aboriginal rights, which included the James Bay and Northern Quebec Agreement and the rights of the Eeyouch in regard to health and social services. However, the Canadian and Quebec governments have often acted as though the Agreement is only a contractual arrangement, subject to federal and provincial will as to whether the services would be funded or not. For years, the Eeyouch were denied access to various Quebec-funded social programs, which should have been introduced shortly after 1975 and which were and are available to other Quebec reserve Indians and to the province's mainstream residents. The list includes youth protection, group home, community health, home support, daycare, and alcohol and drug abuse programs.

The Cree Board received the funding to deliver some of these as late as 1988, which has contributed to today's extremely big caseloads. Throughout the 1980s and 1990s, the Board struggled through one crisis after another, most of which were the result of gross underfunding from the provincial government (which argues that more funding is needed in transfer payments from the federal government). The extent of this government neglect is staggering. The Grand Council of the Crees launched a court action claiming hundreds of millions of dollars in accumulated, unfulfilled Section 14 obligations, up to 1997.

Integrating Traditional Healing and Modern Medicine

In spite of these challenges, and in spite of the fact that the Eeyouch today experience some serious health and social problems, conditions have improved greatly for the Eeyouch over the past 25 years. Federal records show that, in 1975, the Eeyouch suffered from exceptionally high rates of death due to violence and accidents, circulatory system diseases, and infectious diseases like tuberculosis. Infant mortality was very high and rising. Today, the Eeyouch have the third highest diabetes rate in the world and experience unique, but less common, diseases like Cree leukoencephalitis (inflammation of the white matter of the brain).

Even so, the Cree Board of Health and Social Services of James Bay and its staff can take credit for improved health and social conditions that, in most respects, compare well with other First Nations communities in Quebec. Still, they remain below that of mainstream Quebecers, and this will not change unless governments are prepared to invest in correcting a quarter century of neglect. Ongoing negotiations with the Quebec government are beginning to result in some badly needed funding.

Perhaps the greatest challenge facing the Board now is how to integrate traditional healing with modern medicine. Many Eeyouch have become accustomed to viewing health and healing in terms of "programs and services." The modern medical system—with its machines, drugs, and white-coated practitioners—has almost completely displaced traditional medical practices. The traditional holistic approach to health and

I was fortunate to have been brought up on the land. My parents taught me the values, beliefs, and practices—who I was as a Native person—in a very strong and loving way. Those things were instilled in me from an infant to a five year old. Then I was sent to the residential schools, and all that teaching was removed. I became confused. I lost my identity. My life was in turmoil.

I've been following our Native healing processes for the last four years. I find they are more human. There is more compassion and more heart in it. Traditional healing practices have a lot to do with people understanding who they are, including being more in tune with their hearts and souls as human beings.

Nellie House, Chisasibi

healing contrasts sharply with the often impersonal scientific approach known as the "medical model."

The Board's medical practitioners—still all non-Crees—were trained in the Western medical schools. Yet over the years they have, by and large, become more open towards traditional medicine. Although traditional medicine cannot replace Western medicine, the two can be complementary. Sceptics would do well to remember that, like modern medicine, traditional medicine is not dangerous if practised properly. Those who still use natural remedies are carrying on a truly ancient technology, and they might not be the only ones to say that no technology can survive hundreds of generations unless it actually works. Western medicine is now beginning to allow for alternative treatments, providing they do not break the principle of "do no harm." Maybe this is the key.

Hard choices continue to be made by the Cree Board, usually on the basis of insufficient funding. Unfortunately, traditional healing practices carry dollar costs in this modern age. To date, the Board and its staff have been adamant that traditional healing is a luxury that can be utilized only when medical services are adequately funded. But when will this ever be? The Eeyou people themselves have to make this decision and hold all the players accountable.

Today, life is more diverse for the Eeyouch than in the past. Survival requires knowing English or French. There are many professions that a person may enter or skills that may be acquired to make a living. The scope for correct behaviour has been broadened. The stereotypes and role models from Eeyou traditional society are not universally accepted as the young look outside their communities for inspiration and role models.

The knowledge of the elders is too often waning in importance, as the land is destroyed by clear-cutting and by flooding as a result of hydroelectric projects. Environmental destruction and increases in population have closed the door to the hunting way of life for many in our society.

The Eeyouch must redefine themselves based on a blend of their traditions and the needs of a new social organization, but it is likely that they will continue to carve out their future based on their traditional values of honesty, perseverance, and respect for others and the environment. Those who go in new directions will be the stereotypes and role models for the generations after them.

The pipe, the sweat, and the powwow have come back. We have legends of these events in our stories, but we never really knew about them. When the elders started to see those coming back, they remembered. At that first ceremony we had—the sweat lodges—there was nobody there when we started, but when we opened the door later all these elderly people were around the lodge. We invited them over after the ceremony. They came and joined us at a feast, and they started talking. They'd say, "I've seen this when I was a little boy, or a little girl," or "I used to see my grandfather doing that." Even the powwow they started to recognize, although only a few elders know of these ceremonies that were talked about. Some of them might have practised these ceremonies around their traplines.

Charlie Louttit, Chisasibi

Oujé-Bougoumou: The Place Where People Gather

In the 20th century, the rapid changes and upheaval experienced by the James Bay Crees are nowhere more startlingly obvious than in the history of the Crees of Oujé-Bougoumou. Like other Cree bands in the region, they dispersed into family hunting grounds during the winter months, but returned each summer to lands around Lac Opemiska, where they reunited as a larger group.

This peaceful existence was altered forever beginning in the 1920s when mining exploration began in the region. As the identification of mineral deposits intensified, outsiders established mining camps, settlements, and towns. The Oujé-Bougoumou people were threatened and coerced into abandoning their village sites, which were then bulldozed and destroyed. While they tried many times to settle at a chosen town-site so that they could establish health facilities, a school and permanent housing, each time they were pushed off their site. Dispirited, and fearing for their hunting territories, they ended up no longer reuniting in the summer and living more and more in shacks located along the road in six separate locations.

During the 1950s, the Oujé-Bougoumou Cree were classified as part of the Mistissini Cree, but for the most part they never settled in Mistissini and stayed in the intensively mined Chibougamau area on their traditional lands. On paper, the Oujé-Bougoumou Crees had disappeared and they spent the next three decades living as a fractured group in some of the most squalid conditions in Canada.

Relocations of the Oujé-Bougoumou Crees

Hudson Bay Post
1914–1929

Chibougamau Post
1929–1942

Cedar Bay
1943–1951

Campbell Point
1943–1951

Hamel Island
1950–1952

Swampy Point
1952–1962

Doré Lake
1962–1974

Six Camp Location
1974–1989

Lac Opemiska
1989 to Present

During the negotiations for the 1975 James Bay and Northern Quebec Agreement, Oujé-Bougoumou was omitted from discussions, albeit with the promise of addressing their rights to land and inclusion in the Agreement in the future. Through a supreme effort, and working with the Grand Council of the Crees, they fought for their rights. They made their plight known to Canadians by conducting a well planned public relations campaign—they made presentations to Canadian human rights organizations and at international human rights conferences. In July 1989, in order to bring attention to their situation, the Oujé-Bougoumou Crees blockaded a major forestry road that cut through their traditional lands. The blockade ended with a promise by the governments of Quebec and Canada to negotiate in good faith over the provision of resources to permit the Crees to build their new village.

Oujé-Bougoumou was eventually recognized as a distinct community and was provided the resources to enable them to begin the healing process and regain their past stature as a proud and self-sufficient people. This presented them with a unique opportunity in the history of Canada. Not only would the Oujé-Bougoumou Crees be once again united, they would be intimately involved in the design and construction of their own community—a community that would reflect their priorities, values, and culture and enable them to once again plan a future together.

In the 1980s, people from all over the traditional territory came together at meetings to discuss their plans for the new community. The elders wanted three things for the community:

1) to be respectful of the environment,
2) for the architecture to be culturally relevant,
3) to be economically sound and not dependent on welfare—the community wanted future generations to be independent.

Although the elders did not use the term, what they had outlined was essentially what is known as sustainable development.

To assist in the creation of this new community, Douglas Cardinal, a Blackfoot from Alberta and perhaps Canada's most recognized architect, was hired to design the new community's public buildings (administration office, school, healing centre, church, business office, and youth centre). Mr. Cardinal is known internationally for his design of the Canadian Museum of Civilization in Hull, Quebec. Once again Oujé-Bougoumou overcame considerable odds as Mr. Cardinal, who had then recently completed the Museum of Civilization, was looking for a smaller, more intimate project that built on an Aboriginal vision of community.

Mr. Cardinal brought much more than architectural expertise to the project. He conveyed a distinctive sensitivity and insight into Aboriginal culture in his designs and his buildings became enduring testaments to the strength and vigour of Aboriginal cultures. Perhaps equally important, Mr. Cardinal was able to translate people's dreams and visions into tangible architectural form. Working closely together, the result was an

It was an honour to work with a people who have such a rich culture. Also, you knew that their lives would be changed forever. Previously, they lived in tar-paper shacks.

Once the floodgates were open, everybody had an opinion. I went back to the drawing board numerous times and built four models.

Elders and community leaders envisioned traditional dwellings with modern amenities.

Douglas Cardinal
Architect

unqualified success. The Oujé-Bougoumou village is an example to all Aboriginal peoples of how a sense of community, purpose, and values can be achieved and even the most overwhelming challenges can be overcome through determination, faith, and maintaining a solid cultural basis.

Today, the community of Oujé-Bougoumou is known not only for its beautiful architecture, but also for its unique and innovative approach to providing heating energy to the whole village. A district heating system was designed to heat residences, institutions (school, clinic, administration buildings, etc.), and commercial establishments via underground pipes delivering hot-water heat. The source of the energy? Sawdust!

On the lands near Oujé-Bougoumou there is a sawmill that processes wood harvested from the territory. Like most mills, its wood waste is burned in a large beehive burner that operates 24 hours a day. This particular mill would pile most of its waste sawdust in huge mounds at the mill site. This visual presence of waste represented two things to the Oujé-Bougoumou Crees. First, it was a constant reminder to them of the constant logging that was making it more difficult for them to continue their traditional way of life. Second, it was in stark contrast to their traditional approach of harvesting only what is required for use, and finding a use for all parts of anything harvested, plant or animal.

By using sawdust as an energy source, the Oujé-Bougoumou district heating system uses alternative energy technology which is designed to be compatible with the Cree philosophy of conservation. This method of heating also has economic and social benefits: the cost of heating is much lower than conventional heating sources (fossil fuels and electricity) and maintaining the district heating system provides local employment. The dreams of the Crees to live in a community that visually and practically represents their values has been achieved in Oujé-Bougoumou.

A New Definition of Human Settlements

Oujé-Bougoumou Chief Abel Bosum, speaking at the United Nations in September 1995 when Oujé-Bougoumou received a "We the Peoples" award in the category of human settlements.

Over the long course of our political struggles, we had the opportunity to give serious thought to the fundamental planning principles and issues which we knew we would face in the construction of a new village. We came to realize very early in the planning of our new village that the process which we were involved in was like having a clean slate, a clean piece of paper upon which we were charged with the responsibility to write the first chapter of our community's future. We were not obliged to build the village in a particular way and we did not have any preconceived ideas about what was the best way to proceed. What we did have was a very profound sense of responsibility which came from the fact that we all realized that we were building our new village not only for ourselves but for the future generations of our people. We realized that for the legacy which we were leaving for the future generations to be a worthy legacy, and one which we could be proud of leaving behind, we could not afford to be short-sighted and that we had to examine very carefully all the possible solutions to our planning problems, especially what may have appeared to be "easy" solutions, to make sure that they would stand the test of long-term appropriateness. Throughout our planning we tried to imagine ourselves looking at our decisions from the perspective of several generations down the road and wondering if our decisions would be viewed as still beneficial then. We knew that we had only one chance to build a new village and we needed to do it right.

In order to give you a true picture of the dynamics at work in our community which made our political and planning successes possible, I must emphasize that there was another factor at play which cannot be overlooked nor underestimated. That factor is the personal strength, determination, and commitment on the part of the individual Oujé-Bougoumou members to undertake the first steps toward their own healing. We decided very early on in our struggles that, in spite of the decades of abuse we had

suffered, we would do whatever it would take personally to deal with a very wide range of personal and social problems which were the result of the impacts of colonialism and the consequent dispossession of parts of our territory, and our alienation and marginalization from the economic, political, and social life of our region. We did this for the sake of our children and for the sake of future generations of Oujé-Bougoumou Crees. It is not an exaggeration to say that if that personal commitment were not present, supported by a renewed and redefined approach to our spiritual needs, then all the other successes would not have been possible.

What we have learned through our experiences is that genuine progress comes when all of the basic factors which comprise human development are addressed and are in harmony. In our case, the determination of our personal commitments made it possible also to honestly and courageously undertake our political struggles. The success of those political struggles then reinforced our personal growth. These changes together then, in turn, created the background upon which we had the strength to undertake daring and innovative community development projects. And these successes further reinforced our personal development and confirmed for us the wisdom of our approach to our political struggles. Successful Aboriginal development requires that we always keep in mind that the Creator gave us hearts to have vision, minds to devise solutions to problems, and hands to build our communities.

In planning the new village, we defined three major objectives which needed to be met. First, our village had to be constructed in harmony with our environment and with the traditional Cree philosophy of conservation. Because of the importance of our traditional way of life, which is land-based, our development needed to be undertaken in a way that was respectful of, and in harmony with, the environment. Because of our reliance on the land and its resources, we must ensure that the land and resources will be available for those who come after us.

Second, our village had to provide for the long-term financial requirements of our people. It would not do simply to construct something which could quickly become a "welfare enclave."

Third, our village had to reflect Cree culture in its physical appearance and in its functions. We were unwilling to simply import a non-Cree version of a village to our territory. The village needed to be truly ours in every sense of the word.

These planning principles reflect the philosophical basis of our traditional way of life. In recent years, this philosophy has come to be referred to as "sustainable development."

Throughout our planning and construction, the community members have participated at every level of decision making and direction setting, from the expression

of hopes, dreams and visions, to decisions on more technical matters involving the direction of construction.

It was on the basis of this set of beliefs that we undertook a unique approach to the village architecture, the design of our innovative housing program, and the installation of an appropriate alternative energy system, and devised our current economic development plans.

In order to ensure that the physical appearance of our new village reflected our own cultural heritage, we engaged the services of a renowned Aboriginal architect—Douglas Cardinal—to design the major public institutions in the new village. Mr. Cardinal designed the Canadian Museum of Civilization and is now designing the Museum of the American Indian for the Smithsonian Institution in Washington. Because of his Aboriginal background, we did not need to go through the process of training the outside professional to work with Aboriginal people. He understood this instinctively. He did not attempt to impose his own vision on us but worked intensively to have us express the visions within us which would become the basis for the village architecture. The result has been the establishment of a village which not only can our people relate to, but is of such beauty that it challenges us to live up to the ideals expressed in the architecture.

In the area of housing, it was our intention to avoid the situation in which the vast majority of Aboriginal people in Canada find themselves: with inadequate and inappropriate housing, and saddled with government programs which do not meet Aboriginal housing needs. The community has designed and implemented its own housing program with the objective of addressing the housing needs of all the community members, with an emphasis on individual home ownership. By designing a housing program locally and for the long-term we have developed a model which will result in the community becoming self-sufficient in the area of housing and not dependent upon inadequate governmental programs.

We have also installed a very innovative alternative energy system whereby we take the sawdust from sawmills operating in the region and convert that industrial waste into energy to provide heat and hot water for the entire village.

We had begun, during the lengthy political struggle, to think about the role of alternative energy in our community's future and we were prepared to look at various options. On a major highway going through our traditional territory there is a sawmill which specializes in producing two-by-four lumber for the American market. The mill site contains a large beehive burner which burns wood waste almost 24 hours a day. Additionally, the sawmill piles up most of its waste sawdust in huge mounds—virtual mountains—at the mill site.

The visual presence of this wood waste has always been a reminder to us of the nature of the forestry activities which were making it difficult for us to maintain our way of life, and it has been a sad reflection of the manner in which natural resources are exploited by the industries operating within our territory—taking what is wanted for commercial purposes and leaving the rest to rot. We Crees view this practice as offensive. In our approach to harvesting nature's resources, we find a use for all the parts of the resources we harvest, and we waste very little.

About 15 years ago ... the Canadian Forces [military] base in Chibougamau became scheduled for closure. We visited the base at that time, hoping to purchase some furniture or equipment which could be used by the community. We noticed then that the base contained a district heating system fueled by a diesel generator and we wondered if such a system might be more economical than having each house with its own furnace. We further wondered if it was possible to fuel such a system using the waste sawdust produced by the mills of the region and to heat an entire village this way.

Our biomass-fueled district heating system met the test of our planning criteria. It has become a cornerstone of our community development and continues to be a success.

Our energy system is proof that energy can be generated as if communities and the environment mattered—unlike megaprojects, for instance. It is proof also that the philosophies and traditional practices of Aboriginal peoples are relevant to the establishment of modern, sustainable communities.

We realize also that the viability of our future requires that we embark upon an appropriate and determined effort in the area of economic development. In this respect we are developing projects in the areas of service sector enterprises, sustainable forestry, and culture-based tourism. We have come to the realization that for our future to be secure it will be essential for us to secure the protection and recognition of our traditional access to the lands and resources with our traditional territory. Our capacity to sustain what we have accomplished until now requires it.

Our achievements in constructing our new village are living proof that Aboriginal self-determination works. Give us the tools and the result will be an enormous release of creative energies directed at building healthy sustainable communities.

In 1987, the Economic and Social Council of the United Nations granted recognition to the Grand Council of the Crees as a non-governmental organization in consultative status. For many years now, we have participated in the drafting of the Universal Declaration on the Rights of Indigenous Peoples. The declaration's preamble recognizes that "respect for Indigenous knowledge, cultures, and traditional practices contributes to sustainable and equitable development and proper management of the environment."

We believe that our experience in Oujé-Bougoumou, as well as the experience of many of the recipients of the "We the Peoples" award, bear eloquent testimony to the truth of this statement.

A Modern, Traditional Village

Through hard work and careful planning, the Cree of Oujé-Bougoumou emerged from a state of poverty, becoming a vibrant, internationally recognized community.

A traditional Cree village in the modern day

The village layout, with the large, circular space in the centre, translates traditional values into a contemporary setting. The centre buildings echo the traditional Cree dwelling. The circular centre contains the community's main buildings: the youth centre, elder centre, health services, and church. And the circular layout was favoured for more than cultural reasons—it's convenient and accessible.

The site of a new community

The site beside Lake Opemiska was not the community's first choice. That had been farther north, but provincial and federal governments considered it too expensive to build a road there. Furthermore, the Quebec government was pushing the present site because nearby forests were already clear-cut and mining areas had been exploited, so there would be no potential loss of revenue from resources.

An example to the world

Oujé-Bougoumou was represented at Expo 2000 in Hanover, Germany, since the theme of that exposition was balancing nature, technology, and humankind. Oujé-Bougoumou's district heating system, fueled by sawdust from a local sawmill, is cheap, environmentally friendly and self-sufficient. It costs only $20,000 per year to heat the whole village (in an extremely cold climate). There are also plans for the community to generate its own electricity. And 2000 was the first Expo where there was an Indigenous pavilion separate from the pavilions of each country. Instead of the Native communities being an interesting attraction, they contributed to the main theme of the Expo.

An inspiration to all Aboriginal peoples

Oujé-Bougoumou has had an impact on other Aboriginal communities in Canada. Some are thinking of using a district heating system, especially up north, where importing fuel is very expensive. With this system, employment is created and money stays in the community. Around James Bay and Hudson Bay, the availability of peat offers the possibility of another fuel source. Peat is already used in Europe as a source of fuel.

Working at home

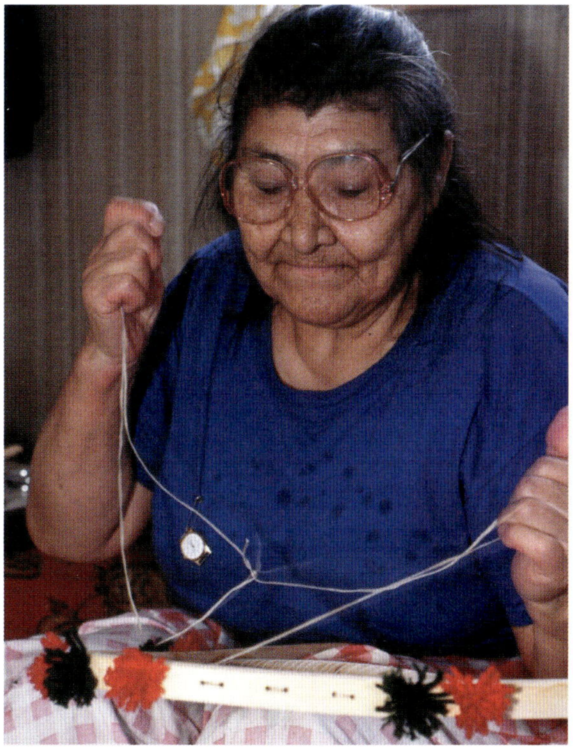

Many Cree are employed in jobs that service and maintain the infrastructure of the community. The Income Security Program provides income to those who undertake traditional pursuits in the bush.

Plans for Oujé-Bougoumou include more cultural tourism, rather than consuming tourist activities such as hunting and fishing. For example, David and Anna Bosum are the owners and operators of Nuuhchimi Wiinuu Cultural Tours. They offer snowshoe and dog-sledding adventures in the winter, and river and lake canoe trips in the summer. All their excursions begin and end at the Cree community of Oujé-Bougoumou, where visitors are given a tour of both the modern and traditional villages.

The community also intends to work on sustainable forestry development and mining for long-term preservation of resources.

Physical
VARSITY
EARTH SYSTEM
WASKAGANISH
QUE

Cree Leaders of Today and Tomorrow

Community Leaders

In 1999, the Crees held an election to replace Matthew Coon Come, Grand Chief of the Grand Council of the Crees, who had led them through the international fight against the Great Whale Project. By a huge majority over other candidates, they chose Dr. Ted Moses. Moses is from Eastmain and for many years had been the Cree ambassador to the United Nations. He began his career as band manager in Eastmain within the administration of Chief Matthew Shanush.

Moses became prominent in the early 1970s as the Cree interpreter in their court case to stop the Province of Quebec's La Grande hydroelectric development project. Later, during the negotiation of the James Bay and Northern Quebec Agreement, he was the chief Cree negotiator. After signature of the Agreement, he became the first Director General of the newly formed Cree School Board and was later elected chief of his own community.

In the early 1980s, at the time of the gastroenteritis epidemic in the Cree communities, the Crees decided to take their treaty rights to the international community. Moses was chosen by the leadership to represent them and to fight for the international rights of Aboriginal peoples. Then when Billy Diamond completed his last term as Grand Chief in 1984, Ted Moses was elected to replace him, a position he held until 1987. Throughout the 1990s, he continued his work in the international arena, becoming a very influential Aboriginal leader at the United Nations.

For his international work on the rights of Aboriginal peoples, the University of Saskatchewan awarded Ted Moses an honorary doctorate of laws in 1996. He was described as having served in "many stressful roles" of Cree leadership—as court interpreter, band manager, teacher, negotiator, chief, director general, grand chief, diplomat, and ambassador. At the ceremony to confer the honorary degree, Chief Leroy Littlebear said of Moses that "his daily struggle to keep internal and Canadian constitutional and human rights respected has been an inspiring example to Indigenous people. In a realm of suspicion, racism, intolerance, and an extravagant hunger for power, Ambassador Moses has proven himself a human of profound decency, tolerance, understanding, humility, and wisdom."

Interviewed in 1999, Moses offered his personal reflections on his years of political involvement and on the 1975 James Bay and Northern Quebec Agreement. The Grand Chief was interviewed again in early 2002, after the Peace of the Brave—the New Agreement between the Crees and the Province of Quebec—had been negotiated. Together, the two interviews offer a personal and historical record of the significant steps taken toward fulfilling an Aboriginal peoples' political dream—self-determination in the development of their communities and economy.

Following the interviews with Grand Chief Ted Moses is an interview with Romeo Saganash, the Grand Council of the Crees' Director of Quebec Relations. Saganash was interviewed in 2002, after the signing of the New Agreement. Saganash has been involved in Cree politics since his early twenties. He was inspired to study law by James O'Reilly, the lawyer who defended the Crees in the early 1970s in their battle against Quebec's first hydroelectric development incursion into Cree territory. The Crees won their case in the Quebec Superior Court, but the judgment was reversed by the Quebec Court of Appeal. However, this case established that the Crees had rights that should not be ignored. Through the study of law, Saganash saw both the value and the limitations inherent in pursuing legal means to secure Cree rights. He was Deputy Grand Chief from 1990 to 1993, and he has been the Grand Council of the Crees' Director of Quebec Relations since 1995.

What both Moses and Saganash have in common is that they were brought up in the bush life. Their traditional Cree parents were aware of the importance of ensuring that their sons were educated in both the bush and school—for their own sake and for the future of the Cree people.

These leaders talk about their lives and their visions of the Cree future.

Dr. Ted Moses, 49

Grand Chief, interviewed in 1999

I was born at the Nemaska post. There were no clinics in those days. My parents just came off the trapline. They decided to spend the summer at the post. A few weeks after I was born, they paddled back to the trapline. I was in the front of the canoe, carried on my mother's back over the portages. I was raised in my earlier years in the bush, on the trapline. I was about nine when I went off to residential school. It was time for me to learn English. I went down to Moose Factory [Ontario]; stayed there for a number of years.

Because I lived in the bush with my parents, I consider myself to be very articulate in Cree. I can do a speech or make presentations without having to resort to an English word.

When I was in the shower one day they called my name. I said, "Here I am," and they said, "Okay, you're leaving tomorrow morning; you're taking the train and going to Brantford, Ontario." After that I went up to Sault Ste. Marie. I left school when I was 19, went home. Did some work, then did some courses at Ryerson and some studies at McGill.

I became band manager at Eastmain. Then I got a call from Robert Kanatewat, chief of Fort George at the time, and he told me over the bush phone that he would like me to come down and translate in the James Bay court case. I had always been translating for the elders in Eastmain. The late Chief Matthew Shanush and the two councillors in Eastmain didn't speak any English, so I did all the reading and writing of correspondence and translated for them for Indian Affairs. I translated for public meetings and for people coming in and getting the plane.

Crees have gotten back their self-confidence, their self-esteem; they've understood what unity means and the strength it can bring.

In the court case, it was a bit scary because there were all sorts of rules that we weren't familiar with—for example, when the person you were translating for asked you a question but should have been asking the court. But I was quite impressed with the judge (Mr. Justice Albert Malouf). I found him to be a very serious person who listened. Oftentimes it's hard for people to do that. I found him very meticulous; he took notes and he asked questions. Of course, he was a clean judge and he wanted a clean record. He came from a minority and believed that they had a place in society, and he protected minority rights. He had moral values in the work that he did.

Our communities had been run by the Hudson's Bay Company or [by the federal government department that handled] Indian Affairs from down south. When people were still going out onto the land they removed our kids, took us away from our parents. It was part of a cultural assimilation plan. What the [James Bay and Northern Quebec] Agreement brought was self-confidence, without having to buy into the assimilation. People have got to think of their culture and their way of life, and we have the land. The land has provided for us and we can continue our way of life and keep our language. But we still want to be able to accept some things that people in other parts of Canada have as a standard, such as new houses, sewage treatment, and so on.

I think the Agreement at that time was well thought out, considering the circumstances and considering the pressures we were under. I don't know if I can really call it a mistake, by the idea of having Aboriginal title extinguished, as a non-negotiable clause for the government at that time. On the other hand, the project was already going on. A road was going through with the construction projects, workers. We were seeing what was going to happen for the next 40 or 50 years, for our lifetime. They've never stopped building.

Now I speak out against extinguishment because I think it's a violation of international human rights. There's no other group that is subjected to that kind of policy; nobody else has to extinguish their rights in order to receive certain benefits that everybody else has got.

We have to realize where we were at that time. We wanted to get control over our education and health and I think Crees were really the ones who broke new ground and developed policies for Canadian Aboriginal people.

I know some people said we needed the project as a jolt to get us moving. But we didn't need the project. You know Crees have increased in population, they have gotten better educated. Now people's aspirations—I wouldn't say have changed—but now we are talking about not only controlling our own education and health but trying to influence Canadian or Quebec policy. Then, we wouldn't have had the bargaining power to do that. Considering the bargaining position we were in at the time, we were able to advance these things. Then we really developed very quickly. Most groups in the country would take a hundred years to sort through and get where we are.

We accepted what already existed but tried to make it more compatible with the Crees so that the Crees could do something with it.

I was one of the people involved in the negotiation. We could have said okay, we'll just have a deal on land compensation, remedial works . . . that type of thing. But we brought in many things while we were able to and while the governments were interested. We were going to get as much as we could out of it. It's what you do with it that really matters. I'd say, after the 25 years we've gone through, it's an evolution. It's like raising a young child: first, you're taught how to snare small game and when you are growing up you learn how to snare a lynx, then trap a beaver, then you move on to the moose.

I'm sure we could have more Cree content in the schools. Now that we've developed our communities, including the language, we have TV and radio broadcasts in Cree. People can communicate with each other. It's part of this process of self-confidence. It's no longer a power from outside that tries to make you into something. You know you're a Cree. You have a land, a way of life; you can take off tomorrow and go trapping if you want and nobody is going to bother you. You can use your language. That's part and parcel of preserving the land, the traditions, a way of life.

I've visited the Cree communities and I've talked to the trappers, the elders; they still have a lot of resentment towards the hydro project about the loss of the land. People don't like that. The land that we were raised on and grew up on. There are a certain category of people like trappers and the older people who had a much closer relationship with the land than the younger generation.

People have seen the impact of what has happened. I'm sure there are benefits but the benefits are being held back, governments are stalling. I've been involved in these negotiations for a number of years, and I've seen it in other parts of the country: it's not written government policy but it's current practice. Once they've got a deal, once they've got extinguishment, then they try and go for more, by getting a group to sign off: go away and don't come back no more.

I've seen situations like in Manitoba, the same things that have been directed toward us: they've had an agreement, they've had a similar organization to the Grand Council, and now the governments are trying to break it down, to go around it and weaken

We're not just isolated communities. We have access to the world and we're known around the world and we're recognized. We're one of the strongest Aboriginal nations—people know the Crees. It's because of public awareness.

It's a big challenge to bring Cree values to other people. I think there is some hope. But we are going against a fast-growing stream. A big tidal wave. We have governments who think that protection of the environment and protection of Indigenous rights are at the lower end of the spectrum.

the strength, and then pick them off, band by band. Out of the five bands in northern Manitoba, four have already signed off under the pretense that they are signing a comprehensive agreement. But there's no reference to the main agreement, only the implementation agreement. Every time they deliver something, you sign on the paper to say that they've fulfilled their obligations. I think this is where leaders are wrong: we don't have the right to sign off rights.

We Crees have to be strong, but we are starting to fragment. Different councils are going off in different directions. People are not being listened to; we are not a united and strong nation. The Agreement is there and we can make it work. My approach is to try and have them implement their obligations without putting the Crees in a situation where we have to sign off. So I'm very hesitant about having another agreement on top of the existing agreement. Let's get down to fulfilling that first agreement before we move on to another one. For example, Hydro-Québec promised us 150 jobs in 1986. They never did that. Then they offered the Crees the concept of partnership with jobs. They are offering jobs today and they haven't even delivered on the first round of jobs.

I remember when the only form of communication was to send a letter. Stamps were five cents at the time and you waited for a couple of months before you got a response. There were no telephones, no other means of communication, except to fly out. If it was urgent, there were radiograms, which were expensive, but you had to keep your message short and simple because it was a radio telephone. Now we have telephone, we have teleconference, we have fax machines, we have Internet.

At one point I was talking to an African ambassador; this was when I was lobbying to have a treaty study carried out by the United Nations. I was lobbying the members of the commission and I was getting them documentation. The ambassador said, "Ted, when you first came up to me and you told me that you were a Cree, an Indian, I was shocked by the fact that you are standing in front of me. In my mind there were no more Indians—they were killed off or assimilated. You've informed me that there are over 300 million Indigenous people in the world. I thought they had already disappeared."

If we are not practising the culture, it has no meaning, and we don't have much chance. What the Crees had was the land, a way of life, a group of people who were still practising hunting, fishing and trapping, which had a value and meaning to them. Especially, the spirituality that was attached to this tradition and culture. If we didn't have that, we wouldn't be a community.

A lot of elders and trappers who have come up to me when I've been in meetings have been saying, "We don't want any more hydroelectric development, we don't want any more forestry, we don't want any mining. We don't want to see all the benefits of the land that we've owned going out and serving other people. Is someone trying to make us poor?"

Now we have Hydro-Québec coming in and offering partnership to the Crees and jobs and all of these benefits, but I don't think the people see hydroelectric development as being beneficial to them. Sure, we get some compensation, but all in all, if you add up forestry, hydroelectric development, mining, several billion dollars go out every year. It's a great deal for them when they can give out a one-time payment as compensation to the Crees. And they extinguished our rights. It's a violation of human rights to take a group of people and make them poor.

Dr. Ted Moses, 51

Grand Chief, interviewed February 2002

The New Agreement that we have signed with Quebec, it's a combination of many things—past efforts in international forums, Cree campaigns, roadblocks, and legal battles. The fact that we had filed close to 30 legal proceedings against Quebec was certainly seen as a threat. The differences between the Crees and Quebec were getting wider, and we live in the same province. At some point, you have to stop and ask yourself whether we will let our differences divide us forever.

The hardest part was deciding whether we could try to resolve our disputes. In the end, we showed we would rather negotiate than litigate.

Our New Agreement with Quebec accomplishes much more than I have seen in any other agreement with Aboriginal peoples in Canada. We still have to fight, I have no doubt about that. There is much more to be done. No one is claiming that we have everything we need. But I sincerely believe that the New Agreement will help us solve our job and housing problems. This, by itself, is a huge accomplishment.

Some people would have you believe that traditional Crees are against the New Agreement. Before we signed it, the Grand Council went around to all the communities to listen to the people. During the community consultations, I heard from many traditional people—trappers and elders. They had a lot to say. They have a lot of wisdom, and they are very practical people. With very few exceptions, the elders and the trappers spoke in favour of the New Agreement. They reminded us that the trapping life is not easy. They said that the cost of trapping and the price of furs make it difficult to be a trapper now. They spoke about a time when furs had much greater value. They are sorry that so few young people now hunt, fish, and trap for a living. But they are concerned about the future for our Cree young people. They spoke of their responsibilities for their families and their concern for how the young people would support their families. They want to do what is best for most of the Crees.

It has also been said that I, as Grand Chief, am selling out our Cree culture for money. But when I visited the communities to talk about the New Agreement, people showed me a lot of respect. These people know me and my family. They know that my own family's trapline will be right in the middle of this development. I have thought a lot about this. I could easily have said: "I don't care if this New Agreement saves a huge amount of Eeyou Istchee from flooding. I don't care if it creates jobs for Crees or gives us economic development or housing. I was with my father on our trapline, and I don't want it touched." My family is one of the small number of families that will see flooding on their traplines. So does that mean I should have refused this deal?

We have to decide our future with our minds, not our hearts. I learned that from my late dad, a trapper. Sometimes you have to use your head. You might want something very much. Your emotions might push you; your feelings might try to take over. That's okay when you are in love, or you look out on a beautiful fall morning and feel the power of the Creator. But you have to keep reason in the picture. God gave us our intelligence to use it, to figure things out. We also have to use that part of our being. When we live on the land, we constantly use our minds to observe, to know what to do. We don't allow our intelligence to be drowned by our emotions. We wouldn't make it through one day if we did that on the land.

Why should we have to invest in Hydro-Québec to gain equity in something all of us already own? We already have equity. Our Cree equity is our consent for the diversion of the Rupert River.

When I have said we need money to develop our communities, people have argued that we would have been wiser to invest in Hydro-Québec than to go with this New Agreement. We don't have to invest: we already own the rights. Why else is Quebec seeking Cree consent? Under the New Agreement, we will obtain a direct percentage of Hydro-Québec's resources without any requirement for us to invest directly. With our own source of revenue, we can do whatever we want, including investing in Hydro-Québec.

I've faced a lot of criticism over this New Agreement with Quebec. I used to joke that if you don't try to do anything, you will never get into any trouble. But, no one fights just to be fighting. We have always been fighting for something—full respect for our rights. I used to be criticized for fighting for rights. Some people said, "Forget about rights. You can't eat rights." I always said, "Rights are the only thing you can eat, because if people don't respect your rights, you won't have anything to eat." We need our rights to be respected.

Think about the history of Aboriginal people on this land since the Europeans came. If valuable minerals are found on our land, if trees grow in our territory, or if rivers flow across our lands, our ownership of these resources has not been legally acknowledged. We have been expected to move out of the way of development so that others could enjoy the benefits of the resources on our ancestral lands. It has only been in very recent years that the idea of compensating Aboriginal people has been recognized, and even then compensation for loss was very minimal in comparison to the vast wealth and resources taken away.

So we fight for our rights, and we fight for our lands and our rights to the resources on them. This New Agreement with Quebec, it acknowledges our right to benefit from the wealth of our lands, to participate in and to actually control its development. The Crees are breaking trail again in Canada. No Aboriginal people has ever had an opportunity like the one we have with Quebec. I think Premier [Bernard] Landry really understands who we are and how we fit into Quebec and Canada. At the same time, Quebec is showing its respect for the fundamental principles of international law. You know, this is the only example in Canada of a government authority recognizing and implementing the principles of self-determination that are called for by the United

Nations Human Rights Committee. We have told the United Nations that this Agreement with Quebec represents a significant step forward in the relations between states and Indigenous peoples.

Now, if we could just get the Government of Canada to show the same respect for those same fundamental principles of international law. Like I said, we still have to fight, but in the meantime, we can move ahead with building houses and creating jobs for our people.

Romeo Saganash, 39

Director of Quebec Relations, Grand Council of the Crees, interviewed April 2002

I'm from Waswanipi. I was born in the forest near Waswanipi and I lived the first six years of my life with my family in the bush. By the age of seven I was taken away to residential school. We were 14 in my family and most of us, except the four older ones, were sent to residential schools. I was sent to the one in La Tuque. I believe Matthew Coon Come and Abel Bosum were there as well, during my time. I spent the next 10 years at the residential school in La Tuque, a place between Three Rivers and Chicoutimi [Quebec]. That was probably the most disturbing part of my life. Essentially, you are taken away from your family, taken away from your territory, your culture, your language, and put into a setting that's very unfamiliar and strange for you, especially at that age.

I always wanted to be like my grandfather and my father. I wanted to be a hunter. For the first six years of my life that's what I did. I never wanted to go out of the bush. As a matter of fact, we always stayed in the bush and rarely went to the central village where everybody else gathered during the summertimes. So, that was the objective of my life—to become like my father and my grandfather. But I guess that others felt that was not my destiny and I was sent away to residential school.

At around 16, after my high school years, I came out of the residential school and I went back into the bush for two years before going to college. I spent those two years in the bush with my oldest brother, essentially because I missed the way of life, the Cree way of life. Then I went to college, what they call CEGEP in Quebec, and I did two years of that and then went back to the bush for another year and a half. So, by the time I was 20 I had spent at least half of my lifetime in the bush and half of my lifetime studying.

In 1985 there was a celebration of the 10th anniversary of the signing of the James Bay and Northern Quebec Agreement, and a symposium on the 1975 Agreement was organized in Montreal. I happened to be walking in the community in the fall of 1985 and bumped into the then-chief, Abel Kitchen, and he informed me of this important symposium on the Agreement. He said, "Romeo, I think this would be interesting for you. You should

At La Tuque, I spoke Cree as my first language, the personnel at the residential schools were English-speaking people, but we were at French schools during the daytime. I was still learning Cree in the summer when I was with my parents. So when you have to learn three languages at the same time, you end up learning none of them very well. Nevertheless, I made it to university.

attend and we'll pay for your costs to go." So I went. And at that time I took the decision I was going to attend law school. I had heard about James O'Reilly [the lawyer], who had defended the Crees in court in the early 1970s, during the James Bay battle, and here he was on this panel at the symposium, debating about the role of the courts in the James Bay and Northern Quebec Agreement negotiations. I saw him, I heard him, and I said, that's what I'm going to do. The following September, in 1986, I entered law school at the Université du Quebec à Montreal. I graduated in 1989, and shortly after that I became Deputy Grand Chief of the Grand Council of the Crees.

During that time, when we were waging our political and legal war against the Great Whale development project, the Meech Lake Accord had just died, and there were also negotiations in the context of the Charlottetown Accord. So I think it was an appropriate time for a Cree leader who could speak French. It was important for the Grand Council and the Crees to have someone to express himself or herself in French during that time of turmoil. I guess, to a certain extent, my role was important because of that. I don't necessarily take credit for anything else, but at least for that. When you can communicate in Quebec on these types of issues in the language of the majority of Quebecers, I guess your message is easier for others to understand.

I was Deputy Grand Chief from 1990 to 1993, when Matthew Coon Come was still Grand Chief. For a time, after 1993, I worked as a consultant with other First Nations in Quebec, on Aboriginal constitutional and environmental negotiations and issues. Then I came back in 1995 as the Director of Quebec Relations for the Grand Council, and that's where I am still.

I was not involved in the negotiations to get to the Agreement in Principle for the New Agreement, but I did act as negotiator to get to the final agreement. I was the head negotiator on the forestry file. It was highly technical and very tough negotiations. The counterparts on either side of the table were pretty tough in their positions with respect to this agreement, with respect to what we each wanted around forestry. I was also involved in discussions at the central table whenever it touched on forestry.

I think the most fundamental change is the fact that we will be responsible for our economic and community development. It is a recognition of autonomy for the Crees, but certainly with autonomy come whole aspects of responsibility. So, it is said that self-government and self-determination is a matter of trial and error, and we've embarked on that path. We will surely make mistakes. This New Agreement is not a perfect agreement. A lot of the achievements that we accomplished with this agreement are a result of the past 25 years of work that was carried out and positions that were taken by the Crees in the past. This New Agreement is as much a contribution of Ted Moses today as it is a contribution of Matthew Coon Come and Billy Diamond, and even of Ted's early involvement in the James Bay and Northern Quebec Agreement.

It's a long struggle and this is where we are now. Perhaps in the next 25 years there will be some room for improvement in this agreement as well. Obviously, those who think we should wait for the perfect agreement before signing anything, they'll have to wait for a long time because it never happens. A negotiated agreement is what it is, a "negotiated agreement." It's a matter of give and take and all that.

So, in my view, taking up responsibilities in this new agreement is something that reflects upon the maturity of your society and your people. We know what our problems are, we know what our challenges are, we know where our needs are. We should know by this time what our priorities should be. So we're taking up these responsibilities and it's not a question of whether or not Quebec will implement its obligations under the 1975 Agreement, it's a question of whether the Crees will now fulfill the hopes and dreams and aspirations of their own people. If it doesn't work out, we'll only have ourselves to blame and nobody else. That's what I like about this New Agreement, that's the major change.

What I've said since the time the AIP [Agreement in Principle] was signed in October 2001 is that I saw in Ted Moses enormous leadership and courage and I saw in Premier Bernard Landry a lot of political imagination and courage as well. To do what Ted did, negotiating the AIP, took a lot of leadership, and that's what I like about Ted Moses. That's what leadership is all about, it's what we expect of our leaders. The other thing in all this that I like is not only did Ted know that he was going to get criticized for the way he negotiated the AIP, in secrecy and all that, he knew that between the signing of the AIP and the final agreement, there was going to be consultations and information sessions in the communities to attempt to answer the concerns and the questions that people would have about the agreement. He knew he would face criticism during this consultation process. That fact that Ted knew this and took up the challenge, that also took enormous courage and leadership.

Being able to consult the Crees in their communities, in their language, is something important to the Crees. When we negotiated and signed the 1975 Agreement, I don't think that we really understood what we signed. But this time, I think that the effort that we put into the consultations and meetings in all the Cree communities, I think people had a better understanding of what we were signing this time around. It was a long consultation process for a lot of my people and a lot of our leaders, and I salute their efforts for that. It wasn't easy.

The 1975 Agreement was neither good nor bad. Being the first modern treaty in Canada, it was an important document for all of us. But it's not a matter of whether it was a good document or a bad document. The problem was that the governments had a difficult time implementing the 1975 Agreement. That was the major obstacle, the major problem. Once the governments got what they wanted, back then, after the construction of the La Grande Project, they basically forgot about the Agreement. That's the difficult time we had to get the governments to implement the Agreement, to respect their obligations, to get proper interpretation of the Agreement. It's the result of the lack of implementation and bad faith.

A lot of the concepts and vision of the 1975 Agreement are very progressive. Other elements are very archaic—the provision that talks about the surrender and extinguishment

I would hope that we can achieve the same thing with the federal government as we have with this agreement with Quebec. If we can do the same with the federal government, then we will have completed the circle.

After the signing of the AIP in October, when I was talking to the media people outside the National Assembly, I said that I sure hope that my sons and daughters will not be before your sons and daughters saying the same things and arguing the same things and complaining about the lack of implementation of this agreement.

of Cree rights is an archaic policy that is still being upheld by the Government of Canada. But then, just look at the provisions under Chapter 22 of the Agreement, the Environmental and Social Protection regime. This was in 1975 and already we had incorporated the concept of social protection and environmental assessment of projects. In that sense, it remains a very progressive document for me. The problem, as I said, was the implementation under the provisions of the Agreement.

In a sense, we've attempted to cover all the bases in the New Agreement. What we saw was missing under the 1975 Agreement, we tried to put in this new relationship. Rather than Quebec implementing the economic and community development of our people, we've taken up that responsibility under the New Agreement. We did not have a settlement of dispute mechanism under the first agreement, but we have a standing liaison committee that will try to settle issues and our differences. The things that were missing in the first one, we tried to put in the second agreement.

That's the major challenge that we have before us, both Quebec and the Crees, to properly and adequately implement this New Agreement. Given the nation-to-nation principle that is enshrined in this agreement, I hope that we can work out our differences through the new provisions that we have in this New Agreement. Already we have noticed that the mentality has changed, even with the bureaucracy in Quebec, in their relations with the Crees and the Cree problems.

It's going to take time to get everything into gear, but I think we're on the right path with respect to all this. There are different schedules in the New Agreement, and things will get gradually implemented over the first year. Already we have started to implement some of the forestry provisions through consultations with the local trappers. A lot of committees and boards are being set up under the New Agreement and things are being carried out on both sides, and it's going smoothly. There are no major obstacles yet.

Of course we expect resistance from, for instance, the forestry industry. If you take it from the perspective that this a nation-to-nation agreement, and what the two nations have decided the industry has to follow, then the new measures that will be in place, the new norms and standards that are in the agreement, will have to be respected. I'm confident that the industry will collaborate with the Crees and Quebec in implementing and respecting these new standards that we have established. That's their obligation. I don't think we should renegotiate with the industry as to how these measures can be implemented over a certain period of time. The standards are there, we negotiated them on a nation-to-nation basis, and they have to be followed. We've noticed that the Quebec government has tried to implement similar measures elsewhere in the province, but because of the reluctance and resistance of the forestry industry, the government had to back off. That's something that the government cannot do with this agreement. The industry will have to understand that and collaborate with the Crees and the government to implement these measures.

The Cree Government Working Group has been around for a couple of years. It's a group whose members are appointed by the Grand Council. This group has a mandate to suggest recommendations to adapt our traditional institutions to the challenges of today. In 1974 we created the Grand Council of the Crees for a purpose, to defend Cree rights and interests. Over the years, the Grand Council has evolved, but a lot of the other institutions that we have in Cree territory have not adapted to the changes over the years. In that sense, 27 years after the signing of the 1975 Agreement, I think it is more than appropriate and relevant that we have the Cree Government Working Group to take a serious look at our institutions and to think about how to adapt them to our needs today. This New Agreement with Quebec sort of adds to their mandate. It brings in a whole new context, a whole new perspective from which we have to consider and assess the institutions and adapt them to our contemporary needs.

Sure, we have traditional values, we have traditions and traditional norms that we used in response to the challenges that we had 400 or 1,000 years ago, or even 100 or 200 years ago. But these traditions haven't adapted to the problems and the environment that we are in today. These traditional institutions cannot possibly have the answers to all the problems and challenges that we have today. We are in a completely new context, a completely new environment where there are several other governments that we have to interact with, there is development taking place in the territory, the territory is occupied by others who are not Cree. So, we have to adapt our own institutions, even our traditional ones, to the realities of today. All societies and all peoples on this planet have to go through that eventually. So that's what we have to do. It's not a question of denying or rejecting our traditions, our traditional values, and our traditional institutions. It's just a matter of adapting to a modern setting where we have to strive to survive as a people, a distinct nation, a distinct society.

When we talk about the need for jobs for our youth, we know that many youth will continue to come on the job market for the next while. If we don't do anything in that regard, then we are heading for a major social crisis in our communities. Despite the fact that the Crees are perceived as a fairly developed people compared with other First Nations in this country, because of the 1975 agreement that we signed, if you look at the social, economic and other indicators, you'll notice that our suicide rate is only slightly lower than that of other First Nations, our psychosocial problems are similar, and so on. So, in that respect, nothing really has changed. In my view, that comes from the fact that we never had access to our own resources for our own development. Our development potential was limited to Category 1A reserve lands, and that's it. With very little of our own resources, with no benefits from the development of our own resources in the vast majority of our traditional territory, that's been a problem. When the Government of Canada announced its Healing Fund for First Nations, a fund of $350 million, my first reaction was, well, once you heal these people, what are they going to do then?

I think Crees have this challenge. Given the fact that we still have people who are living the Cree traditional way of life, we will have to strike a balance between those who have chosen this way of life and want to continue it and those who want to get into the mainstream economy and get jobs. The economic development provisions of the New Agreement allow for that. Development in the territory will take place. I believe there is a need for it. But development will have to take place while respecting the environment, and respecting the Cree way of life, which a large percentage of our people still consider important.

That's going to be a major difference in the future. The annual funds that we will be getting will provide for development and opportunities for our young people. Another challenge will come from the outside. A lot of people will be looking at the Crees and seriously looking at how the Cree Nation will fare in the context of this New Agreement and this new direction we have chosen for ourselves. That's an important role, because other First Nations will be looking our way when trying to find solutions for their own people. We've said since the signing of this agreement that we believe that this is the direction that other First Nations should take. The Royal Commission on Aboriginal Peoples recommended this direction when they said that, fundamentally, First Nations people need to have access to their own resources for their own development. That's what modernity is all about. Octavio Paz, a South American author, said that modernity is a question of adapting, adopting and reinventing your way of life. That's what the Crees are doing.

I only can speak for myself, but a lot of us, in a way, by being born Cree and being born Indian, were born into politics. Sadly, our best resources in all our communities, not just the Crees, but across the country, are thrown into politics and never got a chance to do something else, something that they would have preferred, because they are all dragged and thrown into politics. With this New Agreement, some of us can concentrate on what's good for our people, on not being involved in political battles and legal battles with governments but putting our efforts, our energies, our emotions on people and developing our nation and society. It's time to work for ourselves and for our people and not fight and argue all the time with governments. I'm pretty sure that if it hadn't been for our political struggles and legal battles with governments, we'd probably have had more artists and musicians and authors in our communities. But our best resources were all involved in politics because we had no choice. So that's a major change. We'll have more time for our own people, our families, and for this new relationship with Quebec. It will take time and effort to implement this New Agreement properly, but I think this is a major personal change for a lot of us.

In my case, this agreement brings a sense of great relief, especially as Director of Quebec Relations. I have been at this for more than 20 years now. I started working with the Cree organization back in 1981. This is the beginning of a new direction and it's a relief in that sense. The Agreement was signed in February [2002], and we expect that it will be adopted in legislation by the Quebec National Assembly before the summer recess at the end of June [2002].

Final Words
Eyeeshinakoch Anoch

The Present Day

The Eeyouch are still motivated by the life in the bush. Many Cree people work in day jobs only to pay for the equipment they need to go hunting and fishing every opportunity that comes along. The traditional values still motivate the majority of the population. However, our people now also have interests and follow career paths that were not even dreamed of only a few years ago.

Today, approximately one-third of Eeyou families depend on the bush as their primary source of income. Life is not easy for these people, whose average annual income in 1999 was approximately $12,000 (plus the value of the food they harvested). Most of this income is derived from the Income Security Program negotiated as part of the 1975 James Bay and Northern Quebec Agreement. The rationale for the program is not unlike that given for programs offered to French farmers in France, to keep alive traditions important to the spirit of the nation.

In some ways, Eeyou society has a safety net of social programs that serves to help the ones with problems but also demotivates those who have not yet decided on their futures. As a result, there is a high rate of high school drop out, although there are also a large number who return to school after some years of indecision or perhaps of apprenticeship in living in the bush.

In the early 1970s, there were very few who went on to college or university. Today there are over 400 each year who are taking university and college programs. There are now Eeyou lawyers, accountants, geologists, pilots, economic development specialists, teachers, heavy equipment drivers, carpenters, secretaries, health workers, and more.

While the Eeyouch have taken control of their own communities and have continued to live in the bush, they have yet to reap long-term benefits from the development of Eeyou Istchee. Fewer than one percent of those employed in James Bay development initiatives are Eeyouch. The 1975 Agreement promised a regime that would include the Eeyouch as participants in the benefits of development. Finally, that promise is close to being realized through the New Agreement with the Province of Quebec. For 28 years the Cree Nation fought to breathe life and spirit into an agreement that has become the subject of many legal challenges. In 2002, the Crees will be able to put that adversity behind them, and redirect their attention, their energy, and their imaginations to a common effort—to plan for a future that includes their involvement in the development of all their territorial lands.

The future of the Crees is in the wind. It is up to the Crees, Quebecers, and all other Canadians to ensure that the Eeyouch can catch the wind in their sails and take their boat into the seas of the new millennium.

Photo Credits

Special thanks to Fred Cattroll for the many photos he took during the summer of 2000 and for access to his extensive photo library. Also, an additional thanks to Robert Chitty for his contribution to a comprehensive photo library gathered over the last 10 years, of which some images were used throughout this publication.

The following images appear with permission. Below are the official captions provided with the images.

Inside cover:	Antique map, National Archives of Canada, NMC 7330.
Page 6:	Wooden decoy in form of goose called "Nistshekan," Canadian Museum of Civilization, 75-5922.
Page 6–7:	Model of toboggan, Canadian Museum of Civilization, 73-10502.
Page 8:	The Indian women in the photograph were wearing beaded hoods the back of which very nearly touched the ground when they were standing. Fort Albany, James Bay (1865), National Archives of Canada, PA-68286.
Page 9:	Two Cree Indian women wearing apparel typical of their tribe. Chisasibi (Fort George), P.Q. (January 1946), National Archives of Canada, PA-161448; Photographer: Bud Glunz
Page 10:	Wigwams, tents, Indian canvas canoes, and buildings, Rupert House, Q.C., National Archives of Canada, PA-44299.
Page 12:	Tent near Rupert House (ca. 1869), National Archives of Canada, C-075915.
Page 23:	[Dog sled] Rupert House, Mistassini Co., Q.C., National Archives of Canada, C-75903.
Page 24:	Quebec, Rupert House. Buildings, Q.C. (1892), National Archives of Canada, PA-380091; Photographer: A.P. Low
Page 25:	Native Indians, Rupert House, James Bay, Q.C. (July 1927), National Archives of Canada, PA-96745; Photographer: L.T. Burwash
Page 33:	Goose decoy made of willow twigs and grass, Canadian Museum of Civilization, 81-9284.
Page 41:	Pouch with shoulder strap, Canadian Museum of Civilization, 85-7845.
Page 96:	Rupert House. Salt store and forge daalmeyer triplet—open departure (no stop)—time 3 seconds (1870s), National Archives of Canada, C-15041; Photographer: B.R. Boss